THE CHRISTIAN EVANGELIST

Go Therefore and Make Disciples In Your Own Community!
Volume 2

Edward D. Andrews

The Christian Evangelist

Go Therefore and Make Disciples In Your Own Community!

Volume 2

Edward D. Andrews

ISBN-13: **978-0692241394**

ISBN-10: **0692241396**

Christian Publishing House

Cambridge, Ohio

The Christian Evangelist: Go Therefore and Make Disciples In Your Own Community! Volume 2

support@christianpublishers.org

INTRODUCTION Fulfilling Our Responsibility to Evangelize

Matthew 24:14 English Standard Version (ESV)

14 And this gospel of the kingdom will be proclaimed throughout the whole world as a testimony to all nations, and then the end will come.

Of course, Jesus would not have doubted his own words because he had foreknowledge that they would be fulfilled in the whole world before the end came. Jesus would have known that, in time, an army of disciples would eventually respond to the leading of the Holy Spirit. (Ps. 110:3) What would this army of disciples do? They would effectively evangelize the whole world, from their community outward. While we do not know the day, nor the hour of Jesus' return (Mark 13:32), one sign of that return will be true Christianity entering the arena of the evangelism work, in a significant way. While it has yet even to begin, what role can you play in getting it underway?

Keep in mind that Jesus is coming at the day and hour that we do not know. He specifically asks, "When the Son of Man comes, will he find faith on earth?" (Lu 18:8) The closer we get to the day and hour of Jesus' return, the less time we have left to find the souls of those who are rightly disposed to life, not death. John 5:24 says, "Whoever hears my [Jesus'] word and believes him who sent me has eternal life. He does not come into judgment, but has passed from death to life." As evangelists, we are offering to every living person, the world over, the only hope for salvation, Jesus Christ. (Rom 8:24-25; 15:13; 16:19-20)

While it is true that evangelists have written some books over the last 20 years, which recommend that we refocus our energy from the missionary field to our own local communities outward, it has been slow to take hold. The need to get onboard with this objective is imperative, yet many have been slow to respond, if at all. Hence, in view of the work that lies ahead, that of proclaiming the Good News, teaching, making disciples, let us make the best of the time that remains.

We need a tool to help us along the way. The author of this series has penned a book for Christians and their congregation, which will enable them to begin an evangelism program. You can help by reading this book yourself, and then promoting it to your congregation. *THE EVANGELISM HANDBOOK: How All Christians Can Effectively Share God's Word in Their*

Community, is a practical guide (for real life application) in aiding all Christians in sharing biblical beliefs, the Good News of the Kingdom, how to deal with Bible critics, overturning false beliefs, so as to make disciples, as commanded by Christ. (Matthew 28:19-20)

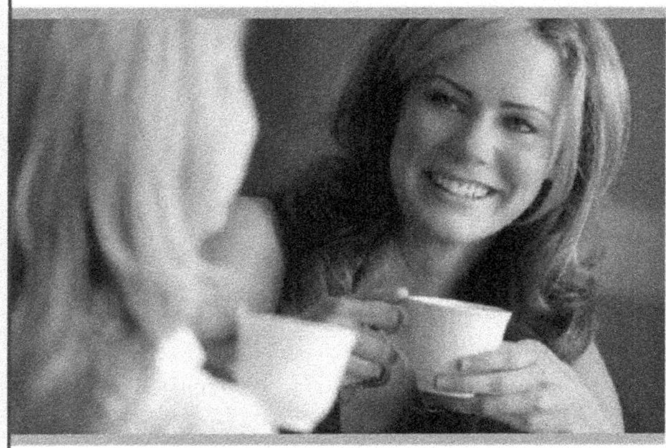

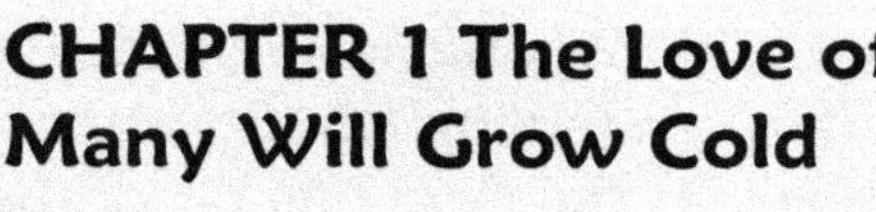

CHAPTER 1 The Love of Many Will Grow Cold

CHAPTER 1

Jesus gave this as one of the signs of the end of the age, "lawlessness will be increased, the love of many will grow cold." (Matt 24:12) There is little doubt that we see this grow rapidly today. These ones refuse to accept the belief (idea or view) of something greater than themselves, and commit acts of violence so horrendous, it hurts the mind to contemplate them.

To mention just one, we look to the "Sandy Hook Elementary School - Newtown, Connecticut (**December 14, 2012**). Adam Lanza, 20, guns down 20 children, ages 6 and 7, and six adults, school staff and faculty, before turning the gun on himself. Investigating police later find Nancy Lanza, Adam's mother, dead from a gunshot wound. The final count is 28 dead, including the shooter."[1]

We can be grateful that Jesus did not say, "The love of **all** will grow cold." We still have tens of millions around the world, who will accept Christ if they are reached by a person,

---

1 http://www.cnn.com/2013/09/19/us/u-s-school-violence-fast-facts/

who has the tools and skills to reason with them from the Scriptures. How should we feel about so many souls that will be receptive to the truth of God's Word, under the right witness?

Be Prepared to Make a Defense

2 Timothy 1:6 English Standard Version (ESV)

6 For this reason I remind you to fan into flame the gift of God, which is in you through the laying on of my hands,

> Having established Timothy's heritage of belief in God and confirmed his conviction that Timothy shared in this genuine faith, Paul issued a command. **For this reason I remind you to fan into flame the gift of God, which is in you.**
>
> The reason Paul could remind Timothy of God's gift was because Timothy was an authentic believer. **The gift of God, which is in you** was probably the Holy Spirit. Every genuine believer receives this gift from God. This is why Paul told Timothy that he was *persuaded* of his sincere faith. Timothy had this powerful

gift within him, enabling him to perform all that God required.

Even so, Timothy must **fan into flame** the Spirit's power. This is a present-tense verb. It might better be translated "keep fanning." It was not that the Spirit's flame was weak or needed to be alive by human effort but that the Spirit only works in cooperation with those who desire his enablement. We keep fanning the flame by keeping "in step with the Spirit" (Gal. 5:25), by disciplining ourselves in godliness to produce the fruit which is his nature (Gal. 5:22).[2]

Romans 12:11 English Standard Version (ESV)

11 Do not be slothful in zeal, be fervent in spirit, serve the Lord.

Here Paul touches a theme mentioned to the Corinthian church after a long exposition concerning the future resurrection of the body, the putting on of immortality for eternity. Though that is not the subject here,

---

[2] The Holman New Testament Commentary http://biblia.com/books/hntc73th/2Ti1.7

> maintaining zeal in service is, especially in the face of persecution or partisanship. He told the Corinthians, "Therefore, my dear brothers, stand firm. Let nothing move you. Always give yourselves fully to the work of the Lord, because you know that your labor in the Lord is not in vain" (1 Cor. 15:58).[3]

In other words, you need to be prepared "to make a defense to anyone who asks you for a reason for the hope that is in you," as well as have the right mindset to help those that will be receptive to the truth. Jesus said that we were 'to find those who are worthy.' (Matt 10:11) All Christians are responsible for proclaiming the good news, teaching the foundational truths of the faith, and making disciples. (Matt 24:14; 28:19-20; Acts 1:8)

Now, what do we do with those, whose **love has grown cold**? These ones are not beyond repentance; therefore, that are able to learn to love again. Those, who were effective evangelists, saved some of those who were angrily opposed to the Christian faith from the fire. We are all obligated to be effective

---

[3] Holman New Testament Commentary http://biblia.com/books/hntc66ro/Ro12.11

evangelists. Some of Christianity's best apologetic defenders came over from being an angry opposer of the faith, because someone won them over. In addition, those who have grown cold also include those who have fallen away from the faith. Some of these can be won over again, as well.

CHAPTER 2 Are You Sharing in the Evangelism Work?

If you are truly a born again Christian, you have the command laid upon you preach (evangelize), teach and make disciples. "Go therefore and make disciples of all nations, ... teaching them to observe all that I have commanded you" (Matt 28:19-20) We should never see this work as being something someone else is supposed to carry out, or that it is a burden to carry. It is not the pastor's responsibility alone, as the obligation is laid upon every Christian.

Ways We Can Share our Faith Within Our Community?

Street Witnessing

The primary method of sharing the Good News in the community is by going house-to-house. However, maybe you are unable to find certain ones at home because they work a shift at the time you are able to go out. Then, there are those that live in gated communities, which you cannot get access to, because there is a restriction against the house-to-house work. In addition, some high-rise apartment buildings do not allow entry but to those who live there, or if you are invited. This means that you are cut off from sharing the message with these ones, as well. This is why witnessing on the street can be quite effective, as we must reach everyone. The most important thing to keep in mind is that this should be carried out in the most respectful way possible, never being aggressive, or have any showy display, such as loud talk, or especially yelling and screaming.

Informal Witnessing

This is sharing the good news with people as you come across them in the community: the store, doctor's office, public transportation, and so on. We are actively to seek out these ones in our everyday activities, such as a fellow employee, a fellow student at school, being served by the server at a restaurant, visiting a friend, and so on. All of these are acts of what is known as an informal evangelism. (John 4:7-15) These are unplanned, but not unprepared occasions where we have an opportunity to share some form of biblical truths (Christian teachings) with another.

This is an effective tool in your evangelism toolbox, in helping them to hear the Good News of God's kingdom. As this facet of witnessing is usually quite brief, one must be prepared with what they might say, and have a Bible tract with them, getting something into their hands before parting ways. On that tract, you should have a way for them to get back with you if they so desire. If you feel things went well enough in this short exchange, you may ask them for some contact information. It takes much courage to approach complete strangers, but it is our love for them, which moves us to buy out the time in this type of evangelism. It is God, who gives "us a spirit not of fear but of power and love and self-control. Therefore, do not be ashamed of the testimony about our Lord."--2 Tim. 1:7, 8

Telephone Witnessing

Small groups of congregation members put to use a reverse phone directory (lists phone numbers by addresses), and go to a small call center that has been set up in the congregation. This is great for getting to people that live in gated communities, or in high-rises that you do not have access to otherwise. Just because we are not face-to-face, does not mean that it is any less effective. In fact, it may be easier on the both because there seems to be less stress. The Christian making the call can have notes in front of him, as well as any research tool, allowing him to field questions. It could be set up so that it works off a desktop computer, with a headset that also has a microphone, leaving the hands free. This is certainly an effective tool.

Remember, this is not the primary way to reach people, but is only a tool for those that you cannot find at home in your community (i.e., the reverse phone directory). The headset should be set up on the computer, so that you can have a splitter plugged in, and multiple people can listen. This way you can train ones, who have done this kind of witnessing. However, it would be best if two people at a time take a call (Luke 10:1). One is the person, who is trying to reach an unbeliever, they could not find at home, and the other is the helper, who looks up information or takes not based on the conversation.

Telemarketing has caused people to shy away from taking calls from anyone they do not know. Therefore, it is best to show feelings of kindness, pleasantness, and tactfulness with your voice. Do not speak too loud, and do not speak to low. You may mention at the outset that you are not selling anything. Use your name, letting them know that you live in their community, and are sharing one Scripture with them and their neighbors. Rather than ask if you can read a Scripture, after stating that is why you have called, just jump to the Scripture, fully citing it and reading it. After reading it, ask a very short open-ended question about the Scripture. If he or she shares their thoughts, keep your word by offering a brief comment and closing out the call. Before hanging up, ask if you may call back this time next week, so you can briefly share another Scripture. On the third or fourth week of doing this, you can begin to engage in more of a discussion. Remember, you will eventually want to visit them in their home, and start a Bible study with them.

Witnessing by Writing Letters

Again, this would be great for getting to people that live in gated communities, or in high-rises that you do not have access to otherwise. Moreover, this would be the approach for one who has a physical disability that keeps them from going out into their community. You can write letters to people within your community, sharing a short biblical thought with them, and enclosing a tract, as well. This is a more relaxed form of evangelism, because you can take your time, to get your words just right, and there is no pressure.

Returning to Evangelize Again

You have made the initial contact with a newly interested one. In the initial discussion, you have planted a couple biblical truths, so you need to return to water these ones, empowering them to grow. (1 Cor. 3:6-8) We now need to get some kind of contact information: phone number, email, or address. You can leave them with a biblical question to ponder, stating what would be the best way to get back with them. Keep in mind that while it may not seem like there is much interest; life is always influencing a person's worldview. Moreover, it is your responsibility to develop interest, as well.

Remember, your end objective is to start a Bible study with ones who are interested. You are always in search of those, who will be receptive to a Bible study. (Matt. 10:11) If you do have one who gives you their contact information, make sure that you get back with them in about a week, because you do not want their interest to fade. In planning your phone call if it was a phone number, or your email, or a visit to their home, make sure you prepare well. Before going the first time, you may have left her or him with a thought provoking question, which you will be addressing this second time. You should have written their name down, and some interesting information that you gleaned from your initial conversation. You will want to use that to show interest in the return.

Your love of God and neighbor keeps this person on your mind until your next contact with them. Once you are on the line with them, or at their home, use their name; try to make the same connection you had the first time around, by spending some time, showing a genuine interest in them. Make them the center of attention by asking open-ended questions that they can answer at length, and be an **active listener** (more on active listening later). In other words, do not be thinking about your next comment or question when a person is talking. An active listener will look at the person while they are talking (not a constant stare, but periodic), and they will move their head in silent agreement or in word, saying quick responses, such as "yeah" or "I see," to let the speaker know that you are listening. If possible, show that you are empathetic to what they are saying, by responding with something like, "I have felt that way before too." It is permissible to ask short clarifying questions as well, which is another way to help the speaker know you are interested.

Remember that your second contact is all about them, with your interjecting some Scripture in, so they remember; it is God's Word that brought you to them. On the second visit, share at least one Scripture, getting their insights as to what they think, tactfully offering the correct interpretation if they are off the mark. With each visit, keep in mind that you are working toward starting a Bible study with them, and inviting them to the congregation meeting. On the visit where you bring up the possibility of a Bible study, pull out the book you intend to use, and give it to them. Explain to them that the study is free of charge, something that takes place once a week, in the convenience of their home if they like, for 30-60 minutes. Have them turn to the Table of Content in the book and walk through some of the things you would be covering. Again, it is our responsibility to cultivate interest in others. Conversation skills are not something that can be taken in by reading some rules and principles. No, they are learned by implementing those rules and principles repeatedly until you become skillful. The first time you find an uninterested person and you develop interest by way of your conversation skills, it will bring you real joy that you have never felt in your life.

Witnessing to Strangers at Meetings

You should be alert to noticing any new faces at the meetings, going up to them and introducing yourself. You should get to know them as you express that you genuinely hope to see them again, befriending yourself to them. Keep in mind that, if everyone assumes that someone else will carry out this form of witnessing, no one will end up doing it, leaving a newly interested one feeling unwanted.

Witnessing by Our Conduct

Either our conduct can help us to shine light on the truth of God's Word, or we can bring reproach on it. (Titus 2:10) If others outside of your congregation have something good to say about your work in the community, this brings honor and glory to God. (1 Pet. 2:12) This can bring new ones to your congregation, because of what they have heard.

Effective Use of Bible Tracts

If you are to engage another in an effective (adequate or productive) discussion, you have to get the conversation started. Like a good book, or a great magazine article, the beginning will determine if you keep going. What you want to do is get the person's attention immediately. You introduce yourself, and a very brief statement that you are talking to people in your community about the Bible, and then offer a tract visually. Most Bible Tracts have two things in common: (1) the titles are designed to peak interest, and (2) the cover image is designed to leap off the page at you, making you want to read it.

Another facet of offering tracts is their size. In a world where it seems that no one has time for anyone else, these short Bible tools can have an impact. When you offer something with a title and image that will capture the attention (interest) of the listener, your success rates are bound to go up. The best way to offer the tracts is to pick out about 4-6 of your best ones, with eye-opening titles and images. Either spread them out as you would a hand of cards, and show them, or preferably place them in the hands of the person, and ask, "Which one would you like?" Now, they are in his hands; he is looking through them, settles on one, and says, "This one."

Now, of course, you will have meditatively studied every tract that you offer yourself. Therefore, you will have a question lined up that highlight the gist of the tract he chose. After asking it, open the tract, read that paragraph that answers your question, and the Scripture that is cited in it from your Bible. If the listener is very conversational, discuss more of the tract, giving him many opportunities to share in the conversation. Before closing the conversation, let him know that you would love to talk again, and write your contact information on the back of the tract, and ask him for his email or phone number.

CHAPTER 3 Proclaiming the Good News with Sheeplike Ones

When a shepherd notices that one of his sheep has hurt itself, or is hungry, he does not just walk by it. It is as though that sheep is his child, so he stops to give it the tender love and care that it deserves. He checks it over, before carrying it to the water and food that it will need to make a full recovery. When we meet newly interested ones in our evangelism work, we too must care with them with just as much, if not more love, care and concern.

If we are an effective evangelist, we are giving of ourselves, our finances, and out time, to reach those in our community. We share the foundational doctrine of the faith with those who are interested, we overcome critical arguments with those who are misinformed, we overturn false reasoning with those who are mistaken, and we even endure the verbal abuse of those who have closed hearts and minds. In all of this, we are hoping to proclaim, teach, and make disciples. Once we find that interested one, what is next?

We need to see them through the eyes of the Father and Son, who are “patient toward you, not wishing that any should perish, but that all should reach repentance." (2 Pet. 3:9) Therefore, in the self-indulgent world that we live in, if anyone demonstrates the tiniest measure of interest in the faith, we need to reciprocate that interest a thousand fold in them, without smothering them. We need to build patiently on that interest, watering it, so God can make it grow.

If we have a mindset, attitude, outlook like this, we will be more open to the Sheeplike ones that are hidden within the chaos of the world. If one grows despondent after much time in not being able to find interest, he can begin to have a different mindset, which becomes all-encompassing. They will begin to feel as though **all** are uninterested, all are critics, all are unreachable, what is the purpose, and why is God not directing us to the sheep. What we may not realize is, God does not only direct us to the Sheeplike ones, but we are obligated to give a witness to the uninterested, so they have had their day in court, so to speak.

Caring for the Sheeplike Ones

When we find one that is interested, what should we do next? We need to inquire about talking with them again. Do not ask if you can, because that offers them an opportunity to say no. Say, 'when would be the best time of the day for me to talk with you again.' Then we need to gather any contact information that we can. Of course, if we are witnessing to them in their home, or at their door, we have the most important piece of information. In addition, if we are witnessing to them through our phone evangelism, we have the second most important piece of information, and the first, because we would be using a reverse phone directory, which has the address, as well.

What happens next, when we return to talk with them again? We are sociable first, seeing how they have been. If they feel comfortable to go into their lives actively listen, and empathetically pay attention. If they have a problem that they share at length, use the Bible to offer comfort, and even solutions, so they can see the benefits of the Scriptures. If they just quickly go over what has been going on since we last spoke with them; then, we can share a brief, interesting Bible topic that can be covered in a couple minutes. We ask if they have any Bible questions they have ever wondered about, which many usually do. If so, we briefly address those. Now, we ask if this day and time are good for us to return.

When we return, we are sociable and do some chatting, and then go into the real reason of why we are out evangelizing, to start home Bible studies with those, who are interested. We pull out a book like **Bible Doctrine: Essential Teachings of the Christian Faith** by Wayne Grudem and Jeff Purswell (Jul 12, 1999),[4] or **Introducing Christian Doctrine(2nd Edition)** by Erickson, Millard J. and Hustad, L. (Apr 1, 2001), or **AMG Concise Bible Doctrines (AMG Concise Series)** by Towns, Elmer (Oct 30, 2011). You place it in their hands, allowing them to open it to the table of content, and talk about how a home Bible study would take place. If you have not read *The Evangelism Handbook* by this author, see the link in the footnote below.[5]

If they have made it this far, they will likely concede to a study. However, if they beg off from studying, what then? We need to keep coming back, developing more rapport, more trust, and more interest. However, we do not want to lose interest in them, by taking longer to return that we had before. This will make the interested one believe that we are not

---

[4] This book has end of chapter questions for personal application, which makes it optimal as a good study tool.

[5] http://bible-translation.net/page/studying-the-bible-with-a-newly-interested-one

interested and putting them off, because they did not take us up on the study opportunity. We need to make a self-appraisal and then reflect on whether we are allowing an interested one, to go uncared for in this wicked world, one who could be a prospective brother or sister.

God has given us the privilege to carry out this work before the end comes. The one, who has been trained to uncover the interest, even if it is buried beneath criticism and complaint, will discover those with a receptive heart. We are workers of God, and we should never set aside our assignment, for the temporary pleasures of the wicked world that we live. If we have the mind of Christ, we will care for those that show interest, until they no longer show interest.

CHAPTER 4 It Is God, Who Makes It Grow

1 Corinthians 3:6-7 English Standard Version (ESV)

[6] I planted, Apollos watered, but God gave the growth. [7] So neither he who plants nor he who waters is anything, but only God who gives the growth.

When you look around at the beautiful landscapes of one country after another, you are awestruck by its splendor, and know that it is God, who set the laws of nature into motion, which made it grow. Magnificent-imposing trees, lush-flourishing shrubs, and banks of intensely colored flowers surround us. Emerald-green lawns incline down to the meticulously tended banks of a stream bubbling with crystal-clear water. Nothing blemishes the sight before you.

We can transfer this same wonderment over to spiritual growth as well. Certainly, we want ourselves to grow spiritually, but we also want those we engage about God's Word to do the same. We want people that we are evangelizing, also to respond to the biblical truths that we share. Certainly, we will pray to God about producing spiritual growth in ourselves, and the ones we witness to, but we must also work in behalf of those prayers. Maybe you feel as though your role in the spiritual growth of another is not enough. Well, take a moment and see what Paul wrote,

1 Corinthians 3:5-7 English Standard Version (ESV)

[5] What then is Apollos? What is Paul? Servants through whom you believed, as the Lord assigned to each. [6] I planted, Apollos watered, but God gave the growth. [7] So neither he who plants nor he who waters is anything, but only God who gives the growth.

The apostle Paul was the greatest evangelist ever, yet he admits, it is God in the end, who gets the credit for the growth. On one occasion, you may have spoken with a person about God's Word, planting some seeds. On another occasion, it may have been another Christian, who expounded on them seeds, watering them, creating potential for growth. Then, another Christian comes along and generates a personal study with this one, watering the initial seeds even more. Nevertheless, in the end, God gets the credit, for making the growth, as we are not anything in the equation.

Nevertheless, how are we to understand Paul's words, when he says, "neither he who plants nor he who waters **is anything**"? The Good News Translation reads, "The one who plants and the one who waters really do not matter." Did Jesus not say that we are to go and "make disciples"? Therefore, is Paul not treating the planter of biblical truth and the one who waters the truth as a less important part, in this discipleship making?

"Neither he who plants is anything"

First, we have to understand the context behind Paul's words. Paul had been talking about, not the Christian ministry, but the stupidity of following men, as opposed to Jesus Christ. Corinth was divided by some following Paul, others Peter, and still others Apollos. Even those these men were great servants of Christ, they would never have advocated being followed, as some were doing, being given undue importance. Then, there were others, who were elevating these supposed "super-apostles," who were, in fact, "such men [were] false apostles, deceitful workmen, disguising themselves as apostles of Christ." 1 Corinthians 4:6-8; 2 Corinthians 11:4-5, 13

Elevating and venerating men in this way is not a sign of spiritual maturity, but rather fleshly thinking, which creates envy, resentment and conflict. (1 Cor. 3:3-4) Paul shows the importance of such thinking when he says, “there is quarreling among you, my brothers. What I mean is that each one of you says, ‘I follow Paul,’ or ‘I follow Apollos,’ or ‘I follow Cephas,’ or ‘I follow Christ.’” 1 Corinthians 1:11-12

Therefore, when Paul says, “neither he who plants nor he who waters is anything,” he is addressing the fleshly thinking within the Corinthian congregation. In other words, they needed to look to Jesus Christ as the leader of the church, recognizing that all the glory for growth goes to God, not some so-called “super apostles” stirring up strife. The apostles and overseers within the congregation were servants of God’s congregation. Thus, no one deserves to be raised up to a position of prestige or distinction. (1 Cor. 3:18-23) In other words, “The planter and the waterer are nothing compared with him who gives life to the seed. Planter and waterer are alike insignificant, though each shall be rewarded according to his particular work.” 1 Corinthians 3:7, *J.B. Phillips New Testament*.

God's Fellow Workers

Therefore, Paul was not diminishing the importance of Christians who plant and water with biblical truths. He certainly did not mean to convey the idea that we are to have a casual, indifferent or detached attitude, "God will make things grow when he sees fit, and does not need us," meaning that we do not need to be involved in the process, as God will get the job done. Paul was very well aware of the role that we have been assigned, and just how important that part is, because, he went on to say, "For we are God's fellow workers." (1 Cor. 3:9) Therefore, he knew that we have a significant effect on the growth of the Christian congregation.

In fact, Paul was always exhorting Christians to work hard as an evangelist and to develop and increase their abilities as a teacher. He told Timothy in a personal letter to him, "Keep a close watch on yourself and on the teaching. Persist in this, for by so doing you will save both yourself and your hearers." (1 Tim. 4:16) In another letter, he also said,

2 Timothy 4:1-2, 5 English Standard Version (ESV)

1 I charge you in the presence of God and
of Christ Jesus, who is to judge the living and
the dead, and by his appearing and his
kingdom: 2 preach the word; be ready in season
and out of season; reprove, rebuke, and exhort,
with complete patience and teaching. 5 As for
you, always be sober-minded, endure suffering,
do the work of an evangelist, fulfill your
ministry.

Similar to Paul and Apollos, we today are able to have the enormous honor and pleasure of serving as one of “God’s fellow workers.” (1 Cor. 3:9; 2 Cor. 4:1; 1 Tim. 1:12) As such, we are a treasured and cherished addition to God’s workforce. Just as a gardener is well aware that God is behind the beauty if his plants and trees, he also knows that he plays a major part in their growth. There is no difference in the spiritual growth of a newly interested one.

We need to ‘be doers of the word, and not hearers only, deceiving ourselves.’ (Jam 1:22) We should be well aware that “the body apart from the spirit is dead, so also faith apart from works is dead.” (Jam 2:26) While we want to give every ounce of our very being in the work of an evangelizer, both planting and watering, we too must, “Be patient, therefore, brothers, until the coming of the Lord. See how the farmer waits for the precious fruit of the earth, being patient about it, until it receives the early and the late rains." James 5:7

We Have Our Own Part

Paul went on to say, "He who plants and he who waters are one, and each will receive his wages according to his labor." 1 Corinthians 3:8

Are there any special qualifications for those who want to take up gardening? Well, yes and no. If you have no knowledge about gardening, your effectiveness at ending up with an aesthetically, artistically appealing, and engaging garden is highly unlikely. You do have the basic knowledge or skill of cultivating plants, especially flowers, in a greenhouse or garden. True, one could begin by trial and error, i.e., on the job training, gaining knowledge and experience as one goes. What does the idiom *trial and error* mean? It means a method of finding a satisfactory solution or means of doing something by experimenting with alternatives and eliminating failures. Notice that we are eliminating failures along the way. This may be acceptable with plants. However, is it an approach that we would want to take with humans? Do paramedics, nurses, nurse practitioner, and doctors carry out their practice by trial and error?

Those mentioned above are in the medical field, to save lives. Christians are in the field of preaching, teaching, and making disciples, to save eternal lives. A doctor might be likened to a Bible scholar (Ph.D), while a nurse practitioner might be likened to a pastor (MDiv), and a nurse may be likened to an assistant pastor (BS). To whom may the paramedics be likened? They may be likened to the Christian evangelist. They have enough knowledge, skills, and experience to save lives, stabilizing the person, until s/he reaches the hospital, namely the church.

The Christian evangelist should have enough Bible knowledge and evangelism skill to stabilize an unbeliever and eventually get them to the congregation.[6] This would mean a foundational knowledge of the faith, basic knowledge of the Bible itself, and the basics of how to interpret God's Word correctly, with the intention of effectively evangelizing any unbeliever. While the Christian evangelist does

---

[6] While my analogy is not perfect, if it is over analyzed, it must be stated that a Christian evangelist is responsible for the continued spiritual growth, of an unbeliever, even after they start attending meetings.

not need an associates, bachelor, MDiv, or Ph.D in biblical studies, to evangelize his or her community effectively and efficiently, they do need the basics of biblical studies.

Therefore, the congregation, or you as an individual, should study these books as follows,

Basic Bible Interpretation

(1) A BASIC GUIDE TO BIBLICAL INTERPRETATION Understanding the Correct Methods of Interpretation by Edward D. Andrews (April 23, 2014)

Basic Bible Doctrines

(1) Bible Doctrine: Essential Teachings of the Christian Faith by Wayne Grudem and Jeff Purswell (Jul 12, 1999)

(2) Introducing Christian Doctrine(2nd Edition) by Erickson, Millard J. and Hustad, L. (Apr 1, 2001)

(3) AMG Concise Bible Doctrines (AMG Concise Series) by Towns, Elmer (Oct 30, 2011)

Spiritual Growth

(1) Walk Humbly With Your God: Putting God's Purpose First in Your Life by Andrews, Edward D. and Prince, Bruce (Apr 29, 2013)

(2) Read the Bible for Life: Your Guide to Understanding and Living God's Word by Guthrie, George (Dec 2, 2013)

(3) Read the Bible for Life (Workbook) by George H. Guthrie (Jan 3, 2011)

"Do Not Let Your Hands Rest"

Ecclesiastes 11:4 Lexham English Bible (LEB)

4 Whoever watches the wind will not sow;
whoever watches the clouds will not reap.

Ecclesiastes 11:6 Lexham English Bible (LEB)

6 Sow your seed in the morning,
and do not let your hands rest in the evening,
for you do not know what will prosper—
whether this or that, or whether both of them alike will succeed.

We will never be an effective evangelist, with some empty, mechanical scattering of biblical truths. Remember the words of Paul, "whoever sows sparingly will also reap sparingly, and whoever sows bountifully will also reap bountifully." 2 Corinthians 9:6

Proverbs 6:10-11

English Standard Version (ESV)

10 A little sleep, a little slumber,
a little folding of the hands to rest,
11 and poverty will come upon you like a robber,
and want like an armed man.

If we want to be effective evangelists, we need to see beyond planting a few seeds of truth. If the truth is to grow in their heart, effort will be needed on our part. We need to continue to water the seeds we have planted, and continue to plant even more, as well as defending the disciple from false teachers and apostates.

There may be times when we hit bad soil after bad soil, i.e., unreceptive hearts after unreceptive hearts. However, we must stay vigilant, as unexpectedly, we may happen upon the good soil, namely a receptive heart. This will bring us such satisfaction that it will overshadow all of those unreceptive hearts. However, if we are not willing to dig, plant, weed and water, we will have no reaping season.

CHAPTER 5 Does the Love of Christ Compel Us?

2 Corinthians 5:14-15 Holman Christian Standard Bible (HCSB)

[14] For **Christ's love compels us**, since we have reached this conclusion: If One died for all, then all died. [15] And He died for all so that those who live should no longer live for themselves, but for the One who died for them and was raised.

When Paul says, "Christ's love compels us," what does he mean? Does he mean subjectively "Christ's love for us" or objectively "our love for Christ"? We will receive no help from the grammar because it allows for either reading. However, the context gives us our answer. In what follows, Paul focuses on Christ's sacrifice; therefore, it seems best to take Paul's words to mean, "Christ's love for us."

It was Jesus himself, who said, "No one has greater love than this, that someone would lay down his life for his friends." (John 15:13) The ransom sacrifice of Jesus Christ should stir in us, such overwhelming feelings of gratitude and appreciation, compelling us to action. Because of the sacrifice, we have wholeheartedly dedicated our lives to God. We are move to speak to others about God's loving provision for salvation. The love of God and the love of neighbor should control our ministry. Is "Christ's love for [you]" compelling you to have a passionate share in proclaiming the good news, teaching the foundations of the faith, and making disciples? Matthew 24:14; 28:19, 20; Acts 1:8

Christ Died for All

Christ **died for all, then all died** along with him. On another occasion Paul wrote, "I have been crucified with Christ. It is no longer I who live, but Christ who lives in me. And the life I now live in the flesh I live by faith in the Son of God, who loved me and gave himself for me." (Gal 2:20) In both places, Paul is using death pictorially, to describe one's conversion. We should note too that, "all" here does not mean "all" are saved by Jesus' ransom. Christ did die for "all," but for one to benefit from that ransom sacrifice; they must have faith in that ransom sacrifice. John 3:18; 2 Thess. 2:12

What did this ransom sacrifice of Jesus Christ open up to "all"? Whoever trusts in Jesus Christ, will not have to suffer eternal death, but will have eternal life. The Father has given the Son the authority to remove our inherited

Adamic sin, giving us instead, the hope of everlasting life. We are set free from slavery to sin, imperfection, and death. (Heb. 2:14, 15; Rom. 5:21) This is not based mere belief, but rather real heartfelt faith, which "is able to save to the uttermost those who draw near to God through him, since he always lives to make intercession for them." Hebrews 7:25

The Son of man, Jesus Christ, corrected the one man Adam. The effects of Adam's sin and rebellion, sending humanity into sin, old age and death are corrected by Jesus' ransom sacrifice. How is this possible? It is possible because Jesus ransom sacrifice was available for all of Adam's descendants, whom Adam sentenced to a lifetime of slavery to sin, ending with the penalty of death. As the apostle Paul says, "the love of Christ controls us, because we have concluded this: that one has died for all, therefore all have died." (2 Cor. 5:14) For all of humanity were sentenced to death by the actions of Adam, Jesus Christ paid the price with his life, just as Paul wrote,

1 Timothy 2:5-6 English Standard Version (ESV)

[5] For there is one God, and there is one mediator between God and men, the man Christ Jesus, [6] who gave himself as a ransom for

all, which is the testimony given at the proper time.

CHAPTER 6 Are You a Reasonable Evangelist

Titus 3:2 Update American Standard Version (UASV)

[2] to speak evil of no man, not to be contentious, to be reasonable, showing every consideration for all men.

At Titus 3:2, we are exhorted "not to be contentious, to be **reasonable**, showing every consideration for all men." Of course, contextually, this encouragement is applied to how we deal with government officials. However, it would be just as applicable to our dealings with those we are evangelizing. The Greek word (*epiekeis*) has the literal meaning of "yielding," which means that we are not to be rigid or stiff in our dealing with others, but rather flexible.

However, if we are reasonable or flexible in our dealing with others, this does not mean we have to compromise or surrender our position on biblical truth. It also does not mean we back away from those, who may be raising objections. No, we are to be trained in the art of communication, having a Good knowledge of Scripture so that we can seek to skillfully overturn false reasoning. However, if the person does not want to hear about the Bible, making it quite clear, we are to respect them and their free will to do so.--Joshua 24:15

If a person says that they are too busy right now to talk, we need to leave them with something. Thus, we could say, "I will be brief, not more than two or three minutes." If we say this, we need to stay within that timeframe. We can share one simple verse with them, offer a thought on it, and share a Bible tract, offering a few comments about it. All of that can be accomplished in three minutes. As we are parting, mention that our contact information is on the back of the tract, and mention that we would like to visit him on another occasion. Because we have respected his time, he may be more inclined to hear us again. In this, we were reasonable, yielding to the unbeliever's conditions.

When someone says that they are busy, it is a kindness on our part, not to ignore their circumstances, so that we can say what we came to say. Imagine we are at our home, dealing with a crisis, and there comes a knock at the door, some salesperson, trying to get us to buy a subscription to some magazine. We tell them that we are busy, and they just ignore that and go into their canvass. We continue to try to break into their pitch, but to no avail. Finally, we just listen, and say “no thank you” in the end. Would we feel kindly toward one, who had treated us in such a way, who failed to be reasonable, respecting our time? What if we had agreed to a few minutes, and the salesperson agreed to five minutes, but stayed 20 minutes. How would that make us feel?

It is a different story, if we attempt to visit a person repeatedly, who has shown interest in talking to us about the Bible, but has repeatedly said they were busy. This may be the case of a person, who is not interested, but is unable to tell us so. Jesus had said, “And if the house is worthy, let your peace come upon it, but if it is not worthy, let your peace return to you.” (Matt. 10:13) We should directly ask the person like so, “I know you are busy each time I stop; if you are not truly interested, please let me know, as I will not be offended by it.” If we part on respectful terms, when the unbeliever has a life circumstance that moves him or her toward Christ, they will not be reluctant because we were upset at being rejected.

It is troubling to us when someone takes advantage of our kindness, by being pushy. Therefore, it is good for us to be reasonable and not rigid, assuming that they have to be receptive. The same is true of our beliefs, as well. We **do not** want to be rigid, expecting that everyone has to accept them. God has given them a free will to reject him, so remember, they are not rejecting us as they are rejecting God. If we explain ourselves in a simple way, having good teaching methods, as well as a reasonable spirit, those, who are rightly disposed toward life, will understand and eventually receive the Good News.

CHAPTER 7

CHAPTER 7 Evangelizing Our Unbelieving Parents and extended Family

Life in the 21st century can have us so busy that we tend to neglect the most obvious people, who need to hear the Good News, our unbelieving parents or other relatives. In fact, many times, we are concerned with trying to evangelize a stranger, but relatives seem to be forgotten. Maybe we tried to witness to them early on, and simply have not revisited them again. Of course, we should heed the words of the apostle Paul, "'Honor your father and mother' (this is the first commandment with a promise)." (Eph. 6:2)

The one honorable thing that we can do for our unbelieving parents is to help them enter the path of salvation, by getting them to accept Christ. Of course, our knowing them intimately does not mean that we are free to be abrasive, but rather, we should be tactful. We might wonder, 'what can I do to help those in my family to accept Christ?' If we are not living at home, and we live a good distance away, we might email them; always throwing in a few comments about how the Bible, has influenced us. We can do this, on occasions for sending cards. We also might briefly speak of the hope of eternal life, as well. Another approach is to share an appropriate Scripture, with a brief comment, or share an experience we have had. However, we want to season our messages, not inundate them; otherwise, they will come across as preachy.

On the other hand, if we are still living with our parent, this affords us many ways of witnessing to them plainly and evasively. In other words, we could bring up God's word directly from time to time. On the other hand, we could allow some of our actions to speak for themselves. For example, we can silently witness to them, if we regularly studied our Bible, where our unbelieving parents could see us. As we head out to Christian meetings, we could make it a point to say, "Goodbye." It is by our conduct as well that we give a silent witness. We need to be clean morally, mentally, spiritually, and physically. They need to see how the Bible is influencing our lives. They see our being hygienically clean, our room is always clean, we are on time, we do not use foul language, the movies we choose are what a Christian can watch, we are kind, polite, and respectful, for which they will take note. These things and more will bring silent praise from one parent to another.

There are occasions where one might lovingly give their parents a Bible as a gift, or even a book that would help them better to appreciate the Bible.[7] When giving a copy of the Bible, or a book, we should write something very moving on the inside cover. Share with them the appreciation we have for the loving way that we were raised and that it is our greatest hope of spending life together for eternity. (John 17:3) It is the emotional, moving words, which may move the parents into asking more about this hope.

The question that we need to ask ourselves is, 'are we doing all that we can, and are we doing it rightly, to help our loved ones onto the path of salvation, by their accepting Christ?'

---

[7] ***WALK HUMBLY WITH YOUR GOD: Putting God's Purpose First in Your Life*** **by Andrews, Edward D. (Apr 29, 2013)**

CHAPTER 8 Your Word Is Truth

CHAPTER 8

Pilate said to Jesus, "So you are a king?" Jesus answered, "You say that I am a king. For this purpose I was born and for this purpose I have come into the world--**to bear witness to the truth**. Everyone who **is of the truth** listens to my voice." Pilate said to him, "**What is truth?**" (John 18:37-38) Jesus had said earlier,

John 8:31-32 English Standard Version (ESV)

[31] So Jesus said to the Jews who had believed him, "If you abide in my word, you are truly my disciples, [32] and **you will know the truth**, and **the truth will** set you free."

We as Christians, true disciples of Jesus Christ, we can only find the truth, with in the Word of God, i.e., the 66 books of the Bible, 39 Old Testament, and 27 New Testament. Jesus would later say in prayer, to the Father,

John 17:17 English Standard Version (ESV)

[17] Sanctify them in the truth; **your word is truth**.

Sadly, there are billions, who have not been set free by **the truth**. These ones are a slave to themselves (humanism)[8] and "the ruler of this world" (John 14:30), the god of this world [who] has blinded the minds of the unbelievers, to keep them from seeing the light of the gospel of the glory of Christ, who is the image of God." (2 Cor. 4:3-4) This is none other than "the great dragon [who] was thrown down, the serpent of old who is called the devil and Satan, who deceives the whole world; he was thrown down to the earth, and his angels were thrown down with him. For this reason, rejoice, O heavens and you who dwell in them. Woe to the earth and the sea, because the devil has come down to you, having great wrath, knowing that he has only a short time." (Rev. 12:9-12) Yes, even though the Bible has been available for almost 2,000 years, being the bestselling book by far, translated into 2,287, it still has not set these ones free from being slaves of the world.

Many simply do not understand it, which causes them to see no significance in paying attention to a book, that is millenniums old,

---

[8] Humanism is a system of thought that is based on the values, characteristics, and behavior that are believed to be best in human beings, rather than on any supernatural authority.

which they feel was written by men, not inspired by God. It is the purpose of Christian Publishing House, that all people, who are rightly disposed toward life, be able to fully and accurately understand the Word of God, to find **the truth**.

It is for this reason; they have begun to publish two series of publications, **(1)** *Basic Teachings of the Bible: Questions Christians Ask - Biblical Answers*, and **(2)** *The Christian Evangelist: Go Therefore and Make Disciples In Your Own Community*! It is a tremendous privilege, to equip the true Christian community with one publication, which shares the Basic teachings of the Bible, as well as another, which teaches them how to be an effective Christian evangelist.[9] By using these tools, the Christian congregation can help those, who are rightly disposed toward life, in their community, to find the path that leads to the truth.

Each of us, who have truly found the truth, is very thankful to the one, who bought out the time, to put us on the path to life. We think of

---

[9] See also, THE EVANGELISM HANDBOOK: How All Christians Can Effectively Share God's Word in Their Community by Andrews, Edward D. (Dec 11, 2013) *A BASIC GUIDE TO BIBLICAL INTERPRETATION Understanding the Correct Methods of Interpretation* by Edward D. Andrews (Apr 22, 2014)

the apostle Andrew, who "found his own brother Simon and said to him, "We have found the Messiah." (John 1:41) Certainly, we too will want to give our master, Jesus Christ the best of ourselves, learning how to share the truth with all, who are willing to listen.

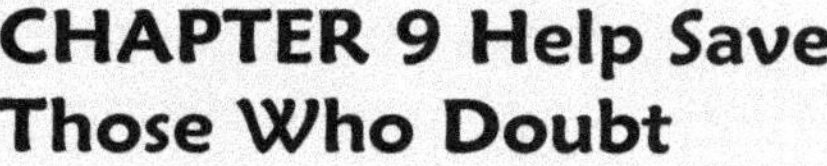

CHAPTER 9 Help Save Those Who Doubt

CHAPTER 9

We certainly live in perilous times, when we think of the crime rates, lawlessness, governments moving toward socialism and communism, terrorism, tens of millions going to be hungry every night, natural disasters, government and big business putting their love of money, position and power before the welfare of the people, a love of pleasure, and the pollution of the earth. Even those, who claim to be rich, are acting just as the apostle Paul said they would, "holding to *a form of godliness*, although they have denied its power." (2 Tim 3:5, italics mine) As we draw ever closer to man destroying man, the need to proclaim the gospel of the kingdom throughout the whole inhabited earth, teaching new ones, making disciples. (Matt. 24:14; 28:19-20)

Beyond all of the above tribulations that face the Christians of the world, there are two that have affected them far greater:

(1) becoming like the world (John 15:19) **[**loving the world (1 John 2:15-17), being a friend of the world (Jam 4:4)**]**, and

(2) the enemies of Christ are more effective at evangelizing the lie, than Christianity is at evangelizing the truth.

What can we do to better prepare the new ones and the spiritually weak one, before doubt begins to overtake them, as it has tens of millions of others? How can we stop the bleeding?

First, the correct process of reading and studying the Word of God is essential to be able to be prepared both offensively and defensively. (Pro 2:1-6; 1 Pet 3:15) Are we consistently attending every Christian meeting each week? Are we preparing for those meetings at home, so that we can have a greater share? Are we digging deeper as we do so? Do we have a personal study aside from what we are being taught at the meetings? Have we formed a longing for these spiritual meals, so that we excited look forward to them, or has our worship become defunct, obligatory, and formalistic?

Second, are we applying the things we have learned? Are we living up to our obligations, as a servant of Jesus Christ? Are we truly loving our neighbor? Is there an evident demonstration of our love for God? Are we having a share in evangelizing our community? Are we doing the one assignment that Jesus gave all Christians?

James 1:22-25 English Standard Version (ESV)

22 But be doers of the word, and not
hearers only, deceiving yourselves. 23 For if
anyone is a hearer of the word and not a doer,
he is like a man who looks intently at his
natural face in a mirror. 24 For he looks at
himself and goes away and at once forgets
what he was like. 25 But the one who looks into
the perfect law, the law of liberty, and
perseveres, being no hearer who forgets but a
doer who acts, he will be blessed in his doing.

Third, do we truly believe the truth of God's Word? Has it affected us inside and out? Are we encouraging love, and helping the Christian congregation toward pur and clean worship, as we await Jesus second coming?

Hebrews 10:24-25 English Standard Version (ESV)

24 And let us consider how to stir up one
another to love and good works, 25 not
neglecting to meet together, as is the habit of
some, but encouraging one another, and all the
more as you see the Day drawing near.

Fourth, has our knowledge of the truth, moved us to share the faith with the unbeliever? Are we encouraging our congregation and those in it, to ramp up the work as the we see the Day drawing near? Is our congregation doing the work that Jesus assigned? If not, have we encouraged such work?

Romans 10:10 English Standard Version (ESV)

10 For with the heart one believes and is justified, and with the mouth one confesses and is saved.

While we want to help unbelievers find the truth, and new ones grow in the faith, and spiritually weak ones get strong, we do not want to manipulate the process, by being pushy, overbearing, or using scare tactics, but rather we want to help those with a pure receptive heart. As Jesus said all too clearly, "out of the abundance of the heart the mouth speaks." (Matt. 12:34) We do not want lip service, unthinking, automatic, mechanical, dutiful persons, but rather those, who are motivated by a heart that truly loves neighbor and God.

Eternal lives are a stake here, so we need to self-analyze ourselves regularly. Am I carried out the will of the Father (Matt 7:21-23)? Am I an effective evangelist? Am I taking my Christian responsibilities seriously? Am I reaching the heart of receptive ones, or is my approach at proclaiming, teaching and making disciples alienating them away? Let us buy out the time in this wicked age, so as to do the work of an evangelist, in the most effective way possible. Let us examine our congregations, and ourselves as each day is, one day closer to the Day.

CHAPTER 10 Why Return to Persons Who Have Shown Interest?

When we share the truth with unbelievers, their interest may be peaked, but to have them be truly interested, some make take more time than others do. If we have spoken to others, persons we do not know, we need to get contact information so that we can make the time to revisit them yet again. We need to cultivate any interest that ones have shown. Just who are we, as Christian evangelists, looking bring into the Christian fold? We are looking for those, who love truth, justice, and righteousness, who are distraught over the injustices of this wicked world.

Luke 19:3-5 English Standard Version (ESV)

3 And he was seeking to see who Jesus was,
but on account of the crowd he could not,
because he was small in stature. 4 So he ran on
ahead and climbed up into a sycamore tree to
see him, for he was about to pass that
way. 5 And when Jesus came to the place, he
looked up and said to him, "Zacchaeus, hurry
and come down, for I must stay at your house
today."

How can we find such ones? One way is by starting informal conversation in our day-to-day life. We might talk of current affairs, the world conditions that surround us, getting their thoughts on these things. We might also make calls to persons, who live within our community. The same is true of our street witnessing, or our house-to-house evangelism program. These initial questions about things that should concern all of us will help us find the common ground, which can lead more serious and regular discussions of biblical truths. In the treacherous world that we live within, we have to approach ones with that in mind as they have every right to be initially cautious of strangers seeking to speak with them. Therefore, we want to develop a rapport that will allow them to have confidence in our motivations for seeking them out. For some, this may take some time, which means that we will have to be patient. We may want simply to make contact with them, be it by email, phone, mail, or visiting their home, from time to time, to talk of the Scriptures, i.e., what they have to offer us now in a practical way, and what they say about our prospective future. If they are receptive to our visits, we should take our time, and never appear as though we need to be somewhere else.

Suppose one who has shown interest, but has been somewhat reluctant, all of a sudden seems to have the time for some in-depth discussions, this may be because we have come at them with a variety of approaches, and one simply has taken root. One approach is to ask leading questions, and let them do most of the talking, leading the conversation with more questions, at the appropriate time. This enables us to find out what is on their mind, their concerns, their interests, their beliefs, and so on. If he wants to talk about the Bible, something he may know very little about, we would not want to attack every one of his misstatements. We should just allow him a chance to air out his thoughts, knowing we will find the best one for the next discussion. We could even leave him with that thought, as we part company, saying, "I would love to talk with you in greater detail next time, about ________." We must remember that our goal is to hearts not arguments.

We must keep in mind that we are bringing **our** disciples into the congregation, but rather they belong to God. Therefore, if we have found interest in someone, and we know another Christian in our church be more effective in reaching his heart, why not humbly invite him or her along.

Lastly, we should never be discouraged by a lack of interest on the part of one who had initially shown interest. Some just do not want to move beyond social conversation, and they like the short visits that we make to their homes. However, when we invite them to the meetings, they beg off. Moreover, when we invite them to a personal Bible study right there in the convenience of their own home, they refuse. Even though this person is not as interested as we had hope, it may just take more time to cultivate their heart, so they see the need of taking the next step. We simply have to do all that we can, by being effective evangelists and teachers, and remember,

1 Corinthians 3:6-7 English Standard Version (ESV)

[6] I planted, Apollos watered, but God gave the growth. [7] So neither he who plants nor he who waters is anything, but only God who gives the growth.

However, the part we lay as an instrument of God is planting truths after we have cultivated hearts, which may include pulling these ones in time, because our time needs to be focused on receptive hearts. Be slow about coming to this conclusion; giving him or her every opportunity.

CHAPTER 11 How to Develop Interest When Evangelizing

Many Christian evangelists may be struggling with gathering and holding the interest of prospective disciples. Do we find that we are struggling even to get a few words into the conversation? Are we being dismissed in the middle of our introduction or right afterwards? If so, let us look to our exemplar, Jesus Christ,

Luke 10:5 English Standard Version (ESV)

[5] Whatever house you enter, first say, 'Peace be to this house!'

Most are thinking, 'this comment will not go over too well today,' and that would be correct. Nevertheless, it gives us the foundation for an introduction, getting us into the Bible discussion we so much desire. They need to see us as their friend, who comes with information that will be encouraging and bring them peace of mind in this wicked world. We could begin with, "I am very pleased that I found you at home. I have brought you a gift today, which I believe will make this day, the best day of your year." This is a friendly opening, which is encouraging regardless of the person. Of course, whatever brief Scriptural message we have, must come across as being beneficial, not superficial. Below are some more introduction that may get us into a good conversation.

Effective Introductions

We could simply start out with asking them, 'how is your day going, I have brought something that will undoubtedly make it even better."

If we notice at the very beginning that he or she is a friendly person, because they are smiling and offering their hand, we might say, "It is so nice to meet someone with a pleasant disposition, which means you are making the best of this stressful world we live in. Would you not agree that there is little in the world where we can find true happiness?" Allow a response, and then share "I have come to bring you even more happiness."

On the other hand, if you clearly see the other that you are about to engage is not I a good mood, say, "I have stopped you today, because we are offering encouraging information, hope for a better future. As you read or listen to the news, there is not much to encourage us into believing life is going to be better for our children or grandchildren. Do you have a very brief moment, so that I might share some good news with you?"

Introductions need to be simple, short, and encouraging. They are designed as stepping-stone into the biblical message that we want to share. We might simply say, "I am a Christian, and we are speaking with our neighbors about some good news. We do this because we love and care for our neighbors."

Jumpstarting with a Subject

The other route into our biblical presentation is by introducing an interesting subject from the start. This will peak their interest. We might say, "We all thought that technology would give us more time, but would you not agree that our lives are even busier than ever, wishing we had more time?" Allow for a response, and then say, "Well, I do have some good news for you, did you know that the Bible actually has counsel on how we can buy out more time? May I share it with you?"

Another approach is to mention a local problem that is affecting their community. We might say, "We would love to hear your insights on ________________, it is greatly impacting our community." People love to offer advice, and letting them speak at length is a way to build rapport. However, if their insights are not even close to being rational, do not attack their thoughts. Simply find an ounce of common ground within them, and move on into the biblical message we prepared. The objective of starting with a local problem was to jumpstart our biblical message, not debate.

Another conversation starter might be, "have you ever contemplated what it might be like to live forever in a perfect world, with a perfect body and mind?"

Work with other Christians in your church, and generate some great conversation starters, based on the biblical message that you are seeking to convey. Then, create a Bible insert, so that it is handy when members are out evangelizing in the community.

Keep in mind that a well-prepared introduction does not mean that a person of interest will not go off in another direction. Do not be so prepared that we are thrown off our mission, because they are not interested in what we came to talk about. Simply be happy that they are willing to talk, and take advantage of whatever subject they want to discuss.

CHAPTER 12 Being a Faithful Evangelist to the Word of God

Readers, this chapter will be a little more technical than what we have had in the past. However, we can handle it, by slowing down, taking our time, and rereading paragraphs if necessary. Seriously, this will be one of the most important chapters; we will read in our series. Lastly, while we recommend the English Standard Version and the New American Standard Bible, know that Christian Publishing House is working on an Updated American Standard Version.

Matthew 11:28-30 English Standard Version (ESV)

[28] Come to me, all who labor and are
heavy laden, and I will give you rest. [29] Take
my yoke upon you, and learn from me, for I
am gentle and lowly in heart, and you will find
rest for your souls. [30] For my yoke is easy, and
my burden is light."

There are very good reasons for us to be committed and unwavering in our service to Christ. The service itself will bring us rest, which will refresh us in coping with life in this wicked world. We will no longer be burdened with the weight of this world. We will learn how to spend our time, abilities and assets in a more balanced manner, but more importantly, in a better service, to the praise and honor of our heavenly Father. Is there not this sense of peace and refreshment when we are at our Christian meetings? If our church has an evangelism program, where they go out into the community together, we will find even more pleasure in associating with loving brothers and sisters. Moreover, our evangelism work will give us a peace of mind and heart, because we will know that we are doing the will of the Father.

I Never Knew You

Matthew 7:21-23 English Standard Version (ESV)

21 "Not everyone who says to me, 'Lord,
Lord,' will enter the kingdom of heaven, but
the one who does the will of my Father
who is in heaven. 22 On that day many will say
to me, 'Lord, Lord, did we not prophesy in
your name, and cast out demons in your name,
and do many mighty works in your name?'
23 And then will I declare to them, 'I never
knew you; depart from me, you workers of
lawlessness.'

There are thousands out there in our community, who would love to have the peace of mind that we enjoy. Are we ready and able to weed through one hundred people, who will reject our message, even some who will verbally abuse us, to find that one right-hearted person?

Many, who know anything about the Bible, are usually familiar with the King James Version, which is quite complicated to understand with its archaic language. Therefore, we want to offer them a modern translation, but a literal one, which is an exact representation of the Hebrew and Greek in English. The preferred translation in our evangelism work is the English Standard Version or the New American Standard Bible. If we use the popular NIV, or worse still some dynamic equivalent translation, such as the New Living Translation, we are offering them interpretive translations. If ever we have the opportunity to carry on a Bible study with them in their home, we would have to continuous say, 'well this should be rendered this way,' so why not just have a translation that is rendered that way?

Translation Philosophy

• Receptor language: the language into which a text written in a foreign language is translated.

• Native language: the original language in which a text is written.

• Dynamic equivalent: a meaning in the receptor language that corresponds to (is "equivalent" to) a meaning in a native-language text (for example, the "heart" as the modern way of denoting the essence of a person, especially the emotions, which for the ancients was situated in the kidneys).

• Dynamic equivalence: a theory of translation based on the premise that whenever something in the native-language text is foreign or unclear to a contemporary reader, the original text should be translated in terms of a dynamic equivalent.

• Functional equivalent: something in the receptor language that differs from what the original text says but that serves the same function in the receptor language (for example, "firstfruits" translated as "special offering").

• Functional equivalence: a theory of translation that favors replacing a statement in the original text with a functional equivalent whenever the original phraseology or reference is obscure for a modern reader in the receptor language.

• Equivalent effect: a translation that aims to produce the same effect on readers of the translation as the original text produced on its native-language readers.

• Formal equivalence: a theory of translation that favors reproducing the form or language of the original text, and not just its meaning. In its stricter form, this theory of translation espouses reproducing even the syntax and word order of the original; the formulas word for word translation and verbal equivalence often imply this stricter definition of the concept.

• Essentially literal translation: a translation that strives to translate the exact words of the original-language text in a translation, but not in such a rigid way as to violate the normal rules of language and syntax in the receptor language.[10]

Interlinear Bible

---

[10] Leland Ryken. The Word of God in English: Criteria for Excellence in Bible Translation (pp. 18-19).

The interlinear Bible page is set up with the left column where you will find the original language text, with the English word-for-word lexical gloss beneath each original language word; generally, the right column contains an English translation like the ESV, NASB, or the NIV. The interlinear translation in the left column and the modern-day English translation in the right column are parallel to each other. This allows the student to make immediate comparisons between the translation and the interlinear, helping one to determine the accuracy of the translation.

The interlinear and the English equivalent in the left column is not generated by taking the English word(s) from the translation on the right, and then placing them under the original language text. Whether we are dealing with

Hebrew or Greek as our original language text, each word will have two or more English equivalents. What factors go into the choice of which word will go under the original language word? One factor is the period in which the book was written: as the New Testament was penned in the first-century, during the era of Koine Greek, as opposed to classical Greek of centuries past, as well as the context of what comes before and after the word under consideration.

Therefore, the translator will use his training in the original language, or a lexicon to determine if he is working with a noun, verb, definite article, adjective, adverb, preposition, conjunction, participle, and so on. Further, say he is looking at a verb, it must be determined what mood it is in (indicative, subjunctive, imperative, etc.), what tense (present, future, aorist, etc.), what voice (active, middle, passive, etc.), what case (nominative, genitive, dative, etc.) gender, person, singular or plural. In addition, the English words under the original language text are generated from grammatical form, the alterations to the root, which affect its role within the sentence, for which he will look to a Hebrew or Greek grammar reference.

The best lexicon is the 3rd *edition Greek-English Lexicon of the New Testament and other*

Early Christian Literature, (BDAG) ten years in the making, this extensive revision of Bauer, the standard authority worldwide, features new entries, 15,000 additional references from ancient literature, clearer type, and extended definitions rather than one-word synonyms. Providing a more panoramic view of the world and language of the New Testament, it becomes the new indispensable guide for translators. The second best lexicon is the Greek-English Lexicon: With a Revised Supplement, 1996: Ninth Revised Edition - Edited By H.G. Liddell, R. Scott By: H.G. Liddell & R. Scott. Each word is given in root form along with important variations, and an excellent representation of examples from classical, Koine, and Attic Greek sources follows. This lexicon is appropriate for all classical Greek and general biblical studies. By far the best traditional Hebrew lexicon currently available is The Hebrew and Aramaic Lexicon of the Old Testament (HALOT) (vols. 1-5; trans. M. E. J. Richardson; Brill, 1994-2000). However, the price is beyond most students and scholars. A more affordable edition, which I highly recommend, is available, Hebrew and Aramaic Lexicon of the Old Testament (Unabridged 2-Volume Study Edition) (2 vols. trans. M. E. J. Richardson; Brill, 2002).

There are numerous lexicons on the market, which would be fine tools for the Bible student. Many scholars would concur that Biblical lexicons have four main weaknesses:

(1) They are geared toward the translations of the 20th century, as opposed to new translations.

(2) They primarily contain only information from the Bible itself, as opposed to possessing information from Greek literature overall.

(3) They are too narrow as to the words of say the New Testament, attempting to harmonize a word and its meaning. The problem with this agenda is that a word can have numerous meanings, some being quite different, depending on its context, even within the same author.

(4) Most Biblical lexicons have not escaped the etymological fallacy, determining the meaning of a word based on its origin and past meaning(s). Another aspect being that the meaning of a word is based on the internal structure of the word. A common English example of the latter is "butterfly." The separate part of "butter" and "fly" do not define

"butterfly." Another example is "ladybird."

John 3:7 (1881 Westcott-Hort New Testament)

[7]me thaumases hoti eipon soi dei humas gennethenai anothen

not to be astonished that I said to you it is necessary you to give birth to from above

[7] Do not be astonished that I said to you, 'It is necessary for you to be born from above.[11]

As we can see the interlinear translation reads very rough, as it is following the Greek sentence structure. The Lexham English Bible rearranges the words according to English syntax. Do not be surprised that at times words may need to be left out of the English translation, as they are unnecessary. For example, The Greek language sometimes likes to put the definite article "the" before personal name, so in the Greek you may have "the Jesus said." In the English, it would be appropriate to drop the definite article, leaving us with "Jesus said." At other times, it may be appropriate to add words to complete the sense in the English translation. For example, at John 4:14, the LEB

[11] W. Hall Harris, III, *The Lexham English Bible* (Logos Research Systems, Inc., 2010), Jn 3:7.

has "But an hour is coming--and now is *here**--when the true worshipers will worship the Father in spirit and truth, for indeed the Father seeks such people to be his worshipers."

*The word "here" is not in the Greek text but is implied, so it is added to complete the sense.

Essential Literal Translation

Once the interlinear level of translation has taken place, it is now time to adjust them into sentences. Each word will possess its own grammatical indicator. As the translator begins to construct his English sentence, he will adjust according to the context of the words surrounding his focus. As you will see shortly, in the examples below, the translator must transition the words from the Greek order, to correct English grammar and syntax. This is the delicate balance faced by the literal translation team. The translation team should actually seek to cling to the Hebrew or Greek word order in our English translation, as far as possible. The reader will find that the KJV, ASV, ESV and the NASB will allow a little roughness for the reader, for them an acceptable sacrifice, as they believe that meaning is conveyed by the word order at times. An overly simplified example might be Christ Jesus as opposed to Jesus Christ, with the former focusing on the office ("Christ" anointed one), while the latter focuses on the person. At times, Greek tends to convey meaning through the word order.

Even though it is impossible to follow the word order of the original in an English translation, the translator will attempt to stay as close as possible to the effective and persuasive use that the style of the original language permits. In other words, what is actually stated in the original language is rendered into the English, as well as the way that it is said, as far as possible. This is why the literal translation is known as a "formal equivalence." As the literal translation, "is designed so as to reveal as much of the original form as possible. (Ray 1982, 47)

It should be noted that this writer favors the literal translation over the dynamic equivalent, and especially the paraphrase. The literal translation gives you what God said, there is no concealing this by going beyond into the realms of what a translator interprets these words as saying. It should be understood that God's Word to man is not meant to be read through like a John Grisham novel. It is meant to be meditated on, pondered over, and absorbed quite slowly; using many tools and helps along the way. There is a reason for this, it being that the Bible is a sifter of hearts. It separates out those who really want to know and understand God's Word (based on their evident demonstration of buying out the opportune time for study and research), from those who have no real motivation, no interest, just going through life. However, there are two weaknesses of the literal translation, if taken too far.

There are times when a literal word-for-word translation is **not** in the best interest of the reader, and could convey a meaning contrary to the original.

(1) As we have established throughout this chapter, but have not stated directly, no two languages are exactly equivalent in grammar, vocabulary, and sentence structure.

Ephesians 4:14 (American Standard Version)

[14] As a result, we are no longer to be children, tossed here and there by waves and carried about by every wind of doctrine, by the trickery [lit., dice playing] of men, by craftiness in deceitful scheming

The Greek word *kybeia* that is usually rendered "craftiness" or "trickery," is literally "dice-playing," which refers to the practice of cheating others when playing dice. If it was rendered literally, “carried about by every wind of doctrine, by the trickery dice-playing of men,” the meaning would be lost. Therefore, the meaning of what is meant by the ‘dice playing’ must be the translator’s choice.

Romans 12:11 (English Standard Version)

[11]Do not be slothful in zeal, be fervent [lit., boiling] in spirit, serve the Lord.

When Paul wrote the Romans, he used the Greek word *zeontes*, which literally means “boil,” “seethe,” or “fiery hot.” Some very serious Bible students may notice the thought of “boiling in spirit,” as being “fervent in spirit” or better “aglow with the spirit,” or “keep your spiritual fervor.” Therefore, for the sake of making sense, it is best to take the literal “boiling in spirit”, determine what is meant by those words, “keep your spiritual fervor”, and render it thus.

Matthew 5:3 (New International Version, ©2011)

[3] “Blessed are the poor in spirit, for theirs is the kingdom of heaven.

Matthew 5:3 (GOD’S WORD Translation)

[3]"Blessed are those who [are poor in spirit] recognize they are spiritually helpless. The kingdom of heaven belongs to them.

This one is really a tough call. The phrase "poor in spirit" carries so much history. Many have written on this phrase over the past 2,000 years. Therefore, even some dynamic equivalent translations are unwilling to translate its meaning, not its words. Personally, this writer is in favor of the literal translation of "poor in spirit." Those who claim to be literal translators should not back away because "poor in spirit" is ambiguous, and there is a variety of interpretations. The above dynamic equivalent translation, God's Word, has come closest to what was meant. Actually, "poor" is even somewhat of an interpretation, because the Greek word *ptōchoi* means "beggar." Therefore, "poor in spirit" is an interpretation of "beggar in spirit." The extended interpretation is that the "beggar/poor in spirit" is aware of his or her spiritual needs, as if a beggar or the poor would be aware of their physical needs.

(2) As we have also established in this chapter a word's meaning can be different, depending on the context that it was used.

2 Samuel 8:3 (Holman Christian Standard Bible)

[3] David also defeated Hadadezer son of Rehob, king of Zobah, who went to restore his control [literally, hand] at the Euphrates River.

1 Kings 10:13 (English Standard Version)

[13]And King Solomon gave to the queen of Sheba all that she desired, whatever she asked besides what was given her by the bounty [literally, hand] of King Solomon. So she turned and went back to her own land with her servants.

Proverbs 18:21 (English Standard Version)

[21] Death and life are in the power [literally, hand] of the tongue, and those who love it will eat its fruits.

The English word "hand" has no meaning outside of its context. It could means, "end of arm," "pointer on a clock," "players of cards," "round in a card game," "part in doing something," "round of applause," "member of a ship's crew," or "worker." The Hebrew word "*yad*," which means "hand," has many meanings as well, depending on the context, as it can mean "control," "bounty," or "power." This one word is translated in more than forty different ways in some translations. Let us look at some English sentences, to see the literal way of using hand, and then add what it means, as a new sentence.

- Please give a big *hand* for our next contestant. Please give a big *applause* for our next contestant.
- Your future is in your own *hands*. Your future is in your own *power*. Your future is in your own *possession*.
- Attention, all *hands*! Attention, all *ship's crew*!
- She has a good *hand* for gardening. She has a good *ability* or *skill* for gardening.
- Please give me a hand, I need some help.
- The copperplate writing was beautifully written; she has a nice hand.

At times, even a literal translation committee will not render a word the same every time it occurs, because the sense is not the same every time. The only problem we have is that the reader must now be dependent on the judgment of the translator to select the right word(s) that reflect the meaning of the original language word accurately and understandably. Let us look at the above texts from the Hebrew

Old Testament again, this time doing what we did with the English word "hand" in the above. It is debatable if any of these verses really needed to be more explicit, by giving the meaning in the translation, as opposed to the word itself.

Who went to restore his *hand* at the Euphrates River – who went to restore his control at the Euphrates River

She asked besides what was given her by the *hand* of King Solomon - she asked besides what was given her by the *bounty* of King Solomon

Death and life are in the *hand* of the tongue - Death and life are in the power of the tongue

Dynamic Equivalent Translation

Translators who produce what are frequently referred to as dynamic equivalent translations, take liberties with the text as presented in the original languages. How so? They either insert their opinion of what the original text could mean or omit some of the information contained in the original text. Dynamic equivalent translations may be appealing because they are easy to read.

However, their very freeness at times obscures or changes the meaning of the original text.

WHAT THE BIBLE DOES NOT SAY	WHAT THE BIBLE DOES SAY
Ecclesiastes 9:8 (New Living Translation) [8] Wear fine clothes, with a splash of cologne! **Ecclesiastes 9:8 (Contemporary English Version)** [8]Dress up, comb your hair, and look your best. **Ecclesiastes 9:8 (New Century Version)** [8] Put on nice clothes and make yourself look good. **Ecclesiastes 9:8 (The Message)**	**Ecclesiastes 9:8 (New American Standard Bible)** [8]Let your clothes be white all the time, and let not oil be lacking on your head. **Ecclesiastes 9:8 (English Standard Version)** [8] Let your garments be always white. Let not oil be lacking on your head. **Ecclesiastes 9:8 (American Standard Version)** [8] Let thy garments be always white; and let not thy head lack oil. **Ecclesiastes**

Dress festively every morning. Don't skimp on colors and scarves.	**9:8 (Holman Christian Standard Bible)** [8] Let your clothes be white all the time, and never let oil be lacking on your head.

Paraphrase Translation

A paraphrase is "a restatement of a text, passage, or work giving the meaning in another form."[12] The highest priority and characteristic is the rephrasing and simplification. Whatever has been said in the above about the dynamic equivalent can be magnified a thousand fold herein. The best way to express the level this translation will go to is to select some paraphrases and set them side-by-side with the dynamic equivalent and literal translations. It is recommended that you read verses 1-4 in the Message Bible, then in the New Living Translation, and then in the English Standard Version. Thereafter, read verses 5-9 in the same manner, followed by verses 10-12, and 13-17. This way you will taste the flavor of each with

---

[12] Inc Merriam-Webster, *Merriam-Webster's Collegiate Dictionary.*, Eleventh ed. (Springfield, Mass.: Merriam-Webster, Inc., 2003).

just a small bit at a time, so you do not lose the sense of the previous one by too much reading.

Isaiah 1:1-17 The Message (MSG)	**Isaiah 1:1-17 New Living Translation (NLT)**	**Isaiah 1:1-17 English Standard Version (ESV)**
[1]The vision that Isaiah son of Amoz saw regarding Judah and Jerusalem during the times of the kings of Judah: Uzziah, Jotham, Ahaz, and Hezekiah. [2-4]Heaven and earth, you're the jury. Listen to God's case: "I had children and	[1] These are the visions that Isaiah son of Amoz saw concerning Judah and Jerusalem. He saw these visions during the years when Uzziah, Jotham, Ahaz, and Hezekiah were kings of Judah. [2] Listen, O heavens! Pay attention, earth! This is what the Lord says:	[1]The vision of Isaiah the son of Amoz, which he saw concerning Judah and Jerusalem in the days of Uzziah, Jotham, Ahaz, and Hezekiah, kings of Judah. [2] Hear, O heavens, and give ear, O earth; for the LORD has spoken: "Children have I reared and brought up, but they have

raised them well, and they turned on me. The ox knows who's boss, the mule knows the hand that feeds him, But not Israel. My people don't know up from down. Shame! Misguided God-dropouts, staggering under their guilt-baggage, Gang of miscreants, band of	"The children I raised and cared for have rebelled against me. 3 Even an ox knows its owner, and a donkey recognizes its master's care— but Israel doesn't know its master. My people don't recognize my care for them." 4 Oh, what a sinful nation they are— loaded down with a burden of	rebelled against me. 3The ox knows its owner, and the donkey its master's crib, but Israel does not know, my people do not understand." 4Ah, sinful nation, a people laden with iniquity, offspring of evildoers, children who deal corruptly! They have forsaken the LORD, they have despised the Holy One of Israel, they are

vandals—
My people have walked out on me, their God,
turned their backs on The Holy of Israel,
walked off and never looked back.

5-9"Why bother even trying to do anything with you
when you just keep to your bullheaded ways?
You keep beating your heads against brick walls.
Everything within you protests

---

guilt.
They are evil people,
corrupt children who have rejected the Lord.
They have despised the Holy One of Israel
and turned their backs on him.

5 Why do you continue to invite punishment?
Must you rebel forever?
Your head is injured,
and your heart is sick.
6 You are battered from head to foot—

---

utterly estranged.

5Why will you still be struck down?
Why will you continue to rebel?
The whole head is sick,
and the whole heart faint.
6 From the sole of the foot even to the head,
there is no soundness in it,
but bruises and sores
and raw wounds;
they are not pressed out or bound up
or softened with oil.

7 Your

against you. From the bottom of your feet to the top of your head, nothing's working right. Wounds and bruises and running sores— untended, unwashed, unbandaged. Your country is laid waste, your cities burned down. Your land is destroyed by outsiders while you watch, reduced to rubble by barbarians.	covered with bruises, welts, and infected wounds— without any soothing ointments or bandages. 7 Your country lies in ruins, and your towns are burned. Foreigners plunder your fields before your eyes and destroy everything they see. 8 Beautiful Jerusalem stands abandoned like a watchman's	country lies desolate; your cities are burned with fire; in your very presence foreigners devour your land; it is desolate, as overthrown by foreigners. 8And the daughter of Zion is left like a booth in a vineyard, like a lodge in a cucumber field, like a besieged city. 9 If the LORD of hosts had not left us a few survivors, we should have

Daughter Zion is deserted— like a tumbledown shack on a dead-end street, Like a tarpaper shanty on the wrong side of the tracks, like a sinking ship abandoned by the rats. If God-of-the- Angel-Armies hadn't left us a few survivors, we'd be as desolate as Sodom, doomed just like Gomorrah. 10"Listen	shelter in a vineyard, like a lean- to in a cucumber field after the harvest, like a helpless city under siege. 9 If the Lord of Heaven's Armies had not spared a few of us, we would have been wiped out like Sodom, destroyed like Gomorrah. 10 Listen to the Lord, you leaders of "Sodom." Listen to the law of our	been like Sodom, and become like Gomorrah. 10Hear the word of the LORD, you rulers of Sodom! Give ear to the teaching of our God, you people of Gomorrah! 11 "What to me is the multitude of your sacrifices? says the LORD; I have had enough of burnt offerings of rams and the fat of well-fed beasts; I do not delight in the blood of bulls,

to my Message, you Sodom-schooled leaders. Receive God's revelation, you Gomorrah-schooled people. 11-12"Why this frenzy of sacrifices?" *God's* asking. "Don't you think I've had my fill of burnt sacrifices, rams and plump grain-fed calves? Don't you think I've had my fill	God, people of "Gomorrah." 11 "What makes you think I want all your sacrifices?" says the Lord. "I am sick of your burnt offerings of rams and the fat of fattened cattle. I get no pleasure from the blood of bulls and lambs and goats. 12 When you come to worship me, who asked you to parade	or of lambs, or of goats. 12"When you come to appear before me, who has required of you this trampling of my courts? 13Bring no more vain offerings; incense is an abomination to me. New moon and Sabbath and the calling of convocations— I cannot endure iniquity and solemn assembly. 14Your new moons and your appointed feasts my soul

of blood
from bulls,
lambs, and
goats?
When you
come before
me,
whoever
gave you the
idea of acting
like this,
Running here
and there,
doing this
and that—
all this
sheer
commotion
in the place
provided for
worship?

13-17"Quit
your worship
charades.
I can't
stand your
trivial
religious
games:
through my
courts with all
your
ceremony?
13 Stop
bringing me
your
meaningless
gifts;
the
incense of
your offerings
disgusts me!
As for your
celebrations
of the new
moon and the
Sabbath
and your
special days
for fasting—
they are all
sinful and
false.
I want no
more of your
pious
meetings.
14 I hate your
hates;
they have
become a
burden to me;
I am weary
of bearing
them.
15 When you
spread out
your hands,
I will hide my
eyes from you;
even though
you make
many prayers,
I will not
listen;
your hands
are full of
blood.
16 Wash
yourselves;
make
yourselves
clean;
remove the
evil of your
deeds from
before my

Monthly conferences, weekly Sabbaths, special meetings—
meetings, meetings, meetings—I can't stand one more!
Meetings for this, meetings for that. I hate them!
You've worn me out!
I'm sick of your religion, religion, religion,
while you go right on sinning.
When you put on your next prayer-performance,
new moon celebrations and your annual festivals.
They are a burden to me. I cannot stand them!
15 When you lift up your hands in prayer, I will not look.
Though you offer many prayers, I will not listen,
for your hands are covered with the blood of innocent victims.
16 Wash yourselves and be clean!
Get your eyes;
cease to do evil,
17 learn to do good;
seek justice,
correct oppression;
bring justice to the fatherless,
plead the widow's cause.

I'll be looking the other way. No matter how long or loud or often you pray, I'll not be listening. And do you know why? Because you've been tearing people to pieces, and your hands are bloody. Go home and wash up. Clean up your act. Sweep your lives clean of your evildoings so I don't have to look at them any	sins out of my sight. Give up your evil ways. 17 Learn to do good. Seek justice. Help the oppressed. Defend the cause of orphans. Fight for the rights of widows.	

longer. Say no to wrong. Learn to do good. Work for justice. Help the down-and-out. Stand up for the homeless. Go to bat for the defenseless.		

Looking at one last example, let us consider the way that one paraphrases Bible translates Jesus' famous model prayer: "Our Father in heaven, reveal who you are." (Matthew 6:9, The Message: The Bible in Contemporary Language) A more accurate translation of Jesus' words renders this passage: "Our Father in the heavens, let your name be sanctified." Note, too, the way that John 17:26 is rendered in some Bibles. According to one free translation, on the night of his arrest, Jesus said to his Father in prayer: "I made you known to them." (Today's English Version) However, a more faithful rendering of Jesus' prayer reads, "I have made your name known to them." Can you see how some translators actually hide the fact that God has a name that should be used and honored?

Literal Contrasted With Dynamic Equivalent

In short, the dynamic equivalent translator seeks to render the biblical meaning of the original language text as accurately as possible into an English informal (conversational) equivalent. Alternatively, the literal translation seeks to render the original language words and style into a corresponding English word and style.

Before we delve into the basics of Bible translation, it would be best to define a couple common acronyms that are commonly used in these sorts of technical discussions. Source Language (SL) is the language from which a translation is being produced in another. Therefore, if one is translating from Hebrew into English, then Hebrew is the SL. Receptor Language (RL) is just the opposite; it is the language into which the translation is being produced. Therefore, if one is translating from Greek into English, then English is the RL.

As you can see from the above, the terms Source and Receptor language have the acronym SL and RL respectively. Also, keep in mind that the text that the translator is rendering into another language is the source text. Please do not confuse the Source Language with the Original Language. True, the Source Language can be the Original Language of say Hebrew or Greek. However, if there is a case of a translator making a Chinese translation of the New Testament, but has chosen to make it from English, the Source Language would be English. Yet, the Original language of the Old Testament is Hebrew, and the New Testament is Greek.

We have the word-for-word and the thought-for-thought. A literal translation is one-step removed from the original and something is always lost or gained, because there will never be 100 percent equivalent transference from one language to the next. A thought-for-thought translation is one more step removed than the literal translation in many cases, and can block the sense of the original entirely. A thought-for-thought translation slants the text in a particular direction, cutting off other options and nuances. A literal word-for-word translation makes every effort to represent accurately the authority, power, vitality and directness of the original Hebrew and Greek Scriptures and to transfer these characteristics in modern English. The literal translations have the goal of producing as literal a translation as possible where the modern-English idiom permits and where a literal rendering does not conceal the thought.

Word-for-Word	**Though-for-Thought**
Literal Translation	Dynamic Equivalent
Focuses on form	Focuses on meaning
Emphasizes source language	Emphasizes receptor language
Translates what was said	Translates what was meant
Presumes original context	Presumes contemporary context
Retains ambiguities	Removes ambiguities
Minimizes interpretative bias	Allows for interpretative bias
Valuable for serious Bible study	Valuable for commentary use

Awkward receptor language style	Natural receptor language style

1 Kings 2:10 Literal Translation (ASV, RSV, ESV, NASB)

And David slept with his fathers, and was buried in the city of David.

And David slept with his fathers, and was buried in the city of David.

Then David slept with his fathers and was buried in the city of David.

Then David slept with his fathers and was buried in the city of David.

1 Kings 2:10 Though-for-Thought Translation (GNB, CEV, NLT, MSG)

David died and was buried in David's City.

Then he died and was buried in Jerusalem.

Then David died and was buried with his ancestors in the City of David.

Then David joined his ancestors. He was buried in the City of David.

One could conclude that the thought-for-thought translations are conveying the idea in a more clear and immediate way, but is this really the case? There are three points that are missing from the thought-for-thought translation:

In the scriptures, "sleep" is used metaphorically as death, also inferring a temporary state where one will wake again, or be resurrected. That idea is lost in the thought-for-thought translation. (Ps 13:3; John 11:11-14; Ac 7:60; 1Co 7:39; 15:51; 1Th 4:13)

Sleeping with or lying down with his father also conveys the idea of having closed his life and having found favor in God's eyes as did his forefathers.

When we leave out some of the words from the original, we also leave out the possibility of more meaning being drawn from the text. Missing is the word *shakab* ("to lie down" or "to sleep"), *'im* ("with") and 'ab in the plural ("forefathers").

Psalm 13:3 American Standard Version

Consider *and* answer me, O Jehovah my God: Lighten mine eyes, lest I **sleep the *sleep of* death**;

John 11:11-14 Updated American Standard Version

This he said, and after that he said to them, "Our **friend Lazarus is fallen <u>asleep</u>**; but I go, that I may awake him out of sleep." The disciples then said to him, "Lord, if he has fallen asleep, he will recover." Now Jesus had spoken of his death, but they thought that he was speaking of literal sleep. Then Jesus told them plainly, "Lazarus has died."

Acts 7:60 American Standard Version

And he kneeled down, and cried with a loud voice, Lord, lay not this sin to their charge. And when he had said this, **he fell asleep**.

1 Corinthians 7:39 Updated American Standard Version

39 A wife is bound for so long time as her husband lives. But if the husband should **fall asleep (*koimethe*) [in death]**, she is free to be married to whom she will, only in the Lord.[13]

1 Corinthians 15:51 American Standard Version

Behold, I tell you a mystery: We all shall not **sleep**, but we shall all be changed,

---

[13] The ASV, ESV, NASB, and other literal translation do not hold true to their essentially literal policy here. This does not bode well in their claim that essential literal is the best policy. I am speaking primarily to the ESV translators, who make this claim in numerous books.

1 Thessalonians 4:13 American Standard Version

But we would not have you ignorant, brethren, concerning them that **fall asleep**; that ye sorrow not, even as the rest, who have no hope.

Those who argue for a though-for-thought translation will say the literal translation "slept" or "lay down" is no longer a way of expressing death in the modern English speaking world. While this may be true to some extent, the context of chapter two, verse 1: """when David was about to die" and the latter half of 2:10: "was buried in the city of David" really resolves that issue. Moreover, while the reader may have to meditate a little longer, or indulge him/herself in the culture of different Biblical times, they will not be deprived of the full potential that a verse has to convey. (Grudem, Ryken, Collins, Polythress, & Winter, 2005, 21-22)

A Word of Caution

The paraphrase and dynamic equivalent can and does obscure things from the reader by overreaching in their translations. This can be demonstrated on the moral standards found in 1 Corinthians 6:9-10.

1 Corinthians 6:9-10 The Message

[9-10] Don't you realize that this is not the way to live? Unjust people who don't care about God will not be joining in his kingdom. Those who use and abuse each other, use and abuse sex, use and abuse the earth and everything in it, don't qualify as citizens in God's kingdom.

1 Corinthians 6:9-10 (English Standard Version)

[9]Or do you not know that the unrighteous will not inherit the kingdom of God? Do not be deceived: neither the sexually immoral, nor idolaters, nor adulterers, nor men who practice homosexuality, [10]nor thieves, nor the greedy, nor drunkards, nor revilers, nor swindlers will inherit the kingdom of God.

If you compare the MSG with the ESV, you will notice that the MSG does not even list the specifics defined by the apostle Paul on precisely what kind of conduct we should shun are not even mentioned.

Matthew 7:13 Today's English Version

[13]"Go in through the narrow gate, because the gate to **hell** is wide and the road that leads to it is easy, and there are many who travel it.

Matthew 7:13 English Standard Version

[13] "Enter by the narrow gate. For the gate is wide and the way is easy that leads to **destruction**, and those who enter by it are many.

The Greek word apōleian means "destruction," "waste," annihilation, "ruin." Therefore, one has to ask, 'why did the TEV translation committee render it "hell"? It has all the earmarks of theological bias.[14] The translation committee is looking to promote the doctrine of eternal torment, not destruction. The objective of the translator is to render it the way that it should be rendered. If it supports a certain doctrine, this should be accepted, if not, then this should be accepted as well. The policy is that God does not need an overzealous translator to convey his doctrinal message.

1 Co. 11:10: LGNTI (Interlinear)

Because of this ought the **woman** authority to have on her head because of the angels

1 Co. 11:10: NASB (Literal)

---

[14] Whether one believes in the hellfire doctrine, i.e., eternal torment, or they are annihilationist, there is one translation principle that they both should favor. We are to translate it accurately. If it favors our doctrinal position, so be it. If it **does not** favor our doctrinal position, so be it. God does not need our help, by twisting the Scriptures to get a desired outcome.

Therefore the **woman** ought to have a symbol of authority on her head, because of the angels.

1 Co. 11:10: TEV (Dynamic Equivalent)

On account of the angels, then, a **woman** should have a covering over her head to show that she is under her husband's authority.

1 Co. 11:10: CEV (Dynamic Equivalent)

And so, because of this, and also because of the angels, a **woman** ought to wear something on her head, as a sign of her authority.

As you can see, the interlinear is completely and literally carried over into the Source Language word for word, keeping the exact form. This is called a **gloss** in the world of the Bible translator. While this does not convey much meaning to the average English reader, it does to one who has studied Biblical Greek. However, the serious Bible student would have a literal translation as a study Bible. The literal translation, as you can see, will keep the form as far as is possible, as well as the wording. The Dynamic Equivalent advocates will argue that this does not sound natural. Well, for those that want the Word of God in its undiluted form, as accurately as possible, we will accept a little unnatural sounding at times. Soon, our example will convey the danger of going beyond translation into interpretation.

Our literal translation contains ambiguity. Is the writer talking about *women* or *wives*? Is the woman to have her own authority, or is something or someone else to have authority over her? This is actually just fine, because its ambiguity has many benefits, as you will see. We have said this in the above, but it is worth repeating again, the work of interpretation will weed out those pseudo-Christians, who do not want to put any effort into their relationship with God, who do not want to buy out the time to understand. Now, the reader has the right to determine for himself or herself which is the correct interpretation. If we do not have an accurate translation, how can we have a correct interpretation? The right of having an accurate translation of the original language should not be stolen from the reader by the translator, for the translator or the committee could be wrong, and life or death may hang in the balance.

Seeing two dynamic equivalents side-by-side helps you to see that they have arrived at two different conclusions and both cannot be right. The *Today's English Version* believes that the "woman" here is really the "wife," as it refers to the "husband." It also believes that the wife is to be under the husband's authority. On the other hand, the *Contemporary English Version* does not commit to the argument of "woman" versus "wife," but does understand the verse to mean the woman has her *own* authority. She has the authority to act as she feels she should, as long as she wears something as a sign of this.

A good translation will do the following:

- Accurately render the original language words and style into the corresponding English word and style that were inspired by God.
- Translate the meaning of words literally, when the wording and construction of the original text allows for such a rendering in the target language.
- Transfer the correct meaning (sense) of a word or a phrase when a literal rendering of the original-language word or a phrase would garble or obscure the meaning.
- In considering the first three points here, as far as possible, use natural,

easy-to-understand language that inspires reading.

Are there such translations available on the market? Yes, this book recommends the following translations below, as every Bible student should have multiple translations, and at least one from every style.

Literal Translations for Bible Study and Research

ESV: *English Standard Version* (2001)

NASB: *New American Standard Version* (1995)

AS V: *American Standard Version* (1901)

Semi-Literal Translations

HCSB: *Holman Christian Standard Bible* (2003)

NET: *New English Translation* (1996)

LEB: *Lexham English Bible* (2010)

Translations Between Literal and Dynamic Equivalent

NIV: *New International Version* (2011)

Dynamic Equivalent Translations

NLT: *New Living Translation* (2004)

CEV: *Contemporary Version* (1995)

TEV: *Today's English Version* (1976)

GNT: Good News Translation (1992)

Paraphrase Translation

MSG: *The Message Bible* (2002)

PHILLIPS: J.B. Phillips New Testament (1962)

TLB: Living Bible (1971)

CHAPTER 13 Knowing When Not to Give the God's Word Away

Proverbs 15:23 English Standard Version (ESV)

23 To make an apt answer is a joy to a man,
and a word in season, how good it is!

Proverbs 25:11 English Standard Version (ESV)

11 A word fitly spoken
is like apples of gold in a setting of silver.

What do we do when we determine that the one we are witnessing to is just not interested? How can we disengage? Should we continue on trying to reach the heart and mind, hoping that we may eventually stimulate interest? Alternatively, would it simply be best to terminate the discussion? It is all about having respect for the person we are trying to evangelize, as well as God himself. We cannot reason with the unreasonable.

Ecclesiastes 3:7 English Standard Version (ESV)

7 a time to tear, and a time to sew;
a time to keep silence, and a time to speak;

Matthew 7:6 English Standard Version (ESV)

[6] "Do not give dogs what is holy [Word of God], and do not throw your pearls before pigs [Word of God], lest they trample them underfoot and turn to attack you.

We must realize that there is a difference between sharing the Good News in an easy to understand way, allowing the listener to determine what his or her reaction will be, as oppose to trying to force the message on someone. We are not sales people, who use pressure tactics to get a sale. We do not force others to accept the truth, as God would not accept anyone, who does not come to him freely.

Joshua 24:15 Updated American Standard Version (UASV)

[15] And if it seems evil to you to serve Jehovah, choose for yourselves today whom you will serve; whether the gods, which your fathers served which were beyond the River, or the gods of the Amorites in whose land you are living; but as for me and my house, we will serve Jehovah.

Our task is to present our message as clearly and understandable as possible so the person knows what we are saying and then he states explicitly that he is uninterested; we can walk away, knowing that we have served God well, and have done our best. Moreover, as we are walking away, we should never view the uninterested (indifferent or apathetic) one as an enemy. In time, life circumstances can alter his outlook, causing him to view things differently. Therefore, a future visit from a fellow Christian may bring about better results. If we leave him respectfully, and he can sense that, he will be more open to future discussions. We could say, "I really appreciate your time, maybe another time."

Why do we not press on, what do we gain by not doing so? First, the person we are speaking to will be impressed that we were respectful, as opposed to be pushy. Second, our being reasonable with him, not forcing him to get upset, may make him more inclined toward a future visit.

If we are abruptly shut down with "I am busy," what can we do? We simply offer a brief comment about the lack of time in the modern day world, and give him a Bible tract, saying, "This takes a mere two minutes to read, I hope that you might consider it when you get a moment. Then, we might discuss it at another time."

This person may genuinely have been busy. On the other hand, he may fear a lengthy conversation. Alternatively, he may have had many bad experiences with other Christians, who lacked tact and respect. On the other hand, he may simply feel that his best defense is not letting us get started. However, our respectful (courteous or polite) disposition may leave him impressed, which may cause him to reconsider and talk with us, or at least, be more open in the future.

Just because we have spoken of how to end uneventful witnessing opportunities, this does not mean that we do not ever look for ways to overcome objections. We are not the type to give up easily in our efforts to make disciples, but we are the type to respect no, when they sincerely mean no. The time of a person's life may very well be why they are inclined toward ignoring the Gospel, so we should not be so quick to judge them by this one encounter. Many young people, for example, are not pressed to talk about eternal life, when it seems that they will live forever.

2 Corinthians 5:20 English Standard Version (ESV)

20 Therefore, we are ambassadors for Christ, God making his appeal through us. We

implore you on behalf of Christ, be reconciled to God.

5:20a. Paul's role in the divine plan of reconciliation led him to a remarkable claim. He and his company were **Christ's ambassadors**. "Ambassadors" was a technical political term used in Paul's day that closely parallels our English word "ambassadors." An ambassador represented a nation or kingdom in communication with other nations. Paul had in mind his apostolic call to represent the kingdom of Christ to the nations of the earth. Ambassadors held positions of great honor in the ancient world because they represented the authority of the kings on whose behalf they spoke.

This was also true for Paul as the ambassador of Christ. When he spoke the message of reconciliation, it was **as though God were making his appeal through** him. Rather than speaking directly to the nations of earth, God ordained that human spokespersons would speak for him. As an apostle, Paul had authority to lead and guide the church (2 Cor. 13:3, 10). Yet, this description applies to all who bear the gospel of Christ to others—even to those who do not bear apostolic authority (1 Pet. 4:11). Though we may not present the gospel as perfectly as Paul did, we do speak on God's behalf when we bring the message of grace to others. But Paul and his company were to be received as mouthpieces of God in the most authoritative sense.

5:20b–21. In these verses Paul summarized the content of the message of reconciliation. His summary includes an expression of his heart, an appeal, and an explanation.

First, Paul introduced his message in emotional terms, expressing his heart. He spoke **on Christ's behalf** because he was an ambassador. But as ordinary ambassadors often sought reconciliation between national enemies with intensity, Paul **implore[d]** others to be reconciled to God. The term *implored* (*deomai*) often connotes beseeching or begging. In imitation of the passionate ministry of Christ himself (Matt. 23:37), Paul so desired to see people come to Christ that he thought of his ministry as begging.

Paul did not actually beg people to have saving faith. He spoke metaphorically in an attempt to convey the motivations behind his ministry. Paul appealed to others for their own sake, even when he was firm or harsh. He knew the enemies of God would suffer divine wrath (Eph. 5:6; Col. 3:5–6). For this reason, his ministry was not impersonal or emotionally disconnected. He desired to see people come to Christ, as should all who minister the gospel on Christ's behalf.

Second, Paul summarized the content of his message of reconciliation in a short appeal. His practice was to tell others to **be reconciled to God**. Since Paul had to appeal to others to be reconciled, he did not believe that the work of Christ automatically reconciled every human being to God. Christ's saving work on the cross is sufficient for every human being, but it is effective only for those who believe. As the imperative (**be reconciled**, from *katallasso*) indicates, those who hear the gospel are responsible to believe in Christ in order to become reconciled to God.

Third, Paul explained that sinful people, who are the enemies of God, can be reconciled to God only through Christ and his work on behalf of the human race. Paul summarized Christ's work in two elements. On the one hand, **God made** Christ, **who had no sin, to be sin**. Paul did not mean that Christ actually became a sinner. Throughout his humiliation, Christ remained faithful and righteous. It is likely that Paul followed the Septuagint's practice of using the term *sin* (*harmartia*) as a circumlocution for "sin offering" (e.g., Num. 6:14). The New Testament frequently refers to Isaiah 53in which the Messiah's death is declared to be "an offering for sin" (Isa. 53:10, NRSV). This language stems from the Old Testament sacrificial system and identifies the sacrifice that brought forgiveness to those for whom it was made (Lev. 4:5–10).

In this sense, Christ became the sin offering **for us**—for all who believe in him. In the gospel of the New Testament, salvation comes to enemies of God because Christ himself became the perfect and final substitutionary sacrifice on behalf of those who have saving faith in him.

Paul then pointed to the purpose of Christ's sacrifice. It was **so that in him we** (all who have saving faith) **might become the righteousness of God**. Note first that it is **in him** (in Christ) that reconciliation takes place. The concept of "in Christ" formed one of Paul's central teachings. To be "in Christ" was to be joined with him in his death and resurrection and thus to receive the benefits of his salvation. In this passage Paul summarized the benefits received in Christ by stating that the believer becomes **the righteousness of God**.

The precise meaning of this expression has been the source of much controversy. Paul probably intended the expression **of God** to be taken as "from God," as Romans 1:17 suggests. Yet, is this righteousness that is infused into believers as they live the Christian life (sanctification)? Or is it the righteousness that is imputed to believers when they turn in faith toward Christ (justification)? Probably Paul's emphasis is on imputed righteousness, since it was by imputation of our sin to Christ, and not by infusion, that Christ was **made … to be sin for us**.

Still, it is best not to divide these issues so sharply as we approach this passage. As Romans 1:17 suggests, the **righteousness from God** is by faith from first to last. Believers become the righteousness from God when they first receive the imputation of Christ's righteousness in justification, but they also receive the continuous blessing of the experience of righteousness in their lives as they grow in their sanctification (cf. Gal. 3:1–5). (Pratt Jr 2000)[15]

---

[15] http://biblia.com/books/hntc67co/2Co5.20-21

CHAPTER 14 Strengthen the Weak Hands

Isaiah 35:3-4 English Standard Version (ESV)

[3] Strengthen the weak hands,
and make firm the feeble knees.
[4] Say to those who have an anxious heart,
"Be strong; fear not!
Behold, your God
will come with vengeance,
with the recompense of God.
He will come and save you."

We can apply this counsel to our helping those new in the faith. We want to assist them every chance we get. One thing that new ones love to do is share their newfound faith with others, but this can be a daunting task for the new one, who is not aware that Satan's henchmen love to pray on the weak. One way you can assist is, by helping them to be prepared for what is to come. Unrealistic expectations on their part, can result in spiritual shipwreck.

The pastor should check in with these new ones often as well, to make sure they are adjusting to their new Christian walk. It can get discouraging if they fall short, when they have not fully overcome some desires of the flesh. Shame and guilt are great tools to keep us securely in our walk, but if they are excessive, with no allowances for human imperfection, they will stumble out of the faith. The pastor can sit down with the new one, and the one who brought the Christian faith to him or her. This way he can make sure their spiritual needs are being met.

Assistant pastors as well are responsible for seeing that the Christian flock is being shepherded. He too needs to make his rounds, making sure everyone's needs are being met. When the assistant pastors take the lead in caring for the duties of the congregation, it gives the pastor more time in his role of shepherding and teaching the flock. (1 Peter 5:2-3)

Everyone enjoys a visit from a friendly face, whose cheerful personality can be upbuilding. It always seems like the encouragement is so timely in a world filled with stresses. New ones should get this from the pastor, assistant pastor and the one, who brought them into the faith. Certainly, we all understand that the world keeps us busy, but let us buy out the time to help those in need of a shepherding call. If you simply stop in for a few minutes, it may not seem like much, but the one receiving the visit will be fully refreshed from your presence, knowing that they are loved.

The irony is, when you give of yourself to others, the deeper joy will be yours. The apostle Paul said, “In all things I have shown you that by working hard in this way we must help the weak and remember the words of the Lord Jesus, how he himself said, ‘It is more blessed to give than to receive.’” (Acts 20:35)

CHAPTER 15

CHAPTER 15 Protect Your Mind and Heart

Psalm 44:18 English Standard Version (ESV)

[18] Our heart has not turned back, nor have our steps departed from your way

All are quite aware what is often termed the greatest killers of the modern day world, cancer and heart disease. However, few are even aware of killers that will end up taking billions of lives, and the lives that they take are eternal lives. Yes, we are talking about Satan and his tens of millions of demons.

Revelation 12:9, 12 English Standard Version (ESV)

[9] And the great dragon was thrown down, that ancient serpent, who is called the devil and Satan, the deceiver of the whole world—he was thrown down to the earth, and his angels were thrown down with him.
[12] Therefore, rejoice, O heavens and you who dwell in them! But woe to you, O earth and sea, for the devil has come down to you in great wrath, because he knows that his time is short!"

The question that begs to be asked is: When does this occur? We know that Satan has had access to the earth from the moment that he tempted Eve in the Garden of Eden. (Genesis 3:1–15; Isaiah 14 and Ezekiel 28) This event of being kicked out of heaven though, is to take place the "time is short" before his being abyssed, i.e., at Jesus second coming. Well, considering that Jesus himself (when on earth) and God's own people do not know the day or the hour of Jesus second coming, Satan surely does not know that time either. However, Satan, a Creature of great power, great intelligence is well aware of the signs that lead us up to the end of the age of this wicked system of things, so he too would be able to grasp when his time was short. Regardless of all this, Satan has had and will have access to us here on earth up unto Jesus' return.

What is Satan's goal? Satan could care less about those, who already reject Christ. He could care less about those forms of Christianity, who are no on the right path, the ones that Jesus is going to say to, "'I never knew you; depart from me, you workers of lawlessness.'" Satan and his tens of millions of demonic angels are concerned with true Christianity, and true Christians. It is their goal, to get every Christian to drift away, to fall away, to turn away, to beg off, to become sluggish, to become hardened to the deceptive power of sin, to tire out, and shrink back to destruction. As the above Psalm states, it should be that our heart never turns back, nor should our steps ever abandon God's way.

Spiritual sickness is the moment Satan loves to attack. All of us succumb to spiritual sickness in our walk with God. It is like getting the common cold. We can take all of the precautions we like, but the unexpected event of being in the wrong place and circumstances is going to lead to us catching a cold. The same is true of the spiritual colds as well. Like any cold, we immediate seek treatment and medications, so that it does not become worse. We have physicians to care for our spiritual sicknesses as well. Our physicians are the Feather, Son and Holy Spirit, "God anointed Jesus of Nazareth with the Holy Spirit and with power. He went about doing good and healing all who were oppressed by the devil, for God was with him." (Acts 10:38)

It is possible for new Christians (Satan's favorite victims), and Christians of many years, who lack spiritual maturity (Satan's second favorite victims), to make their minds over to fortifying their hearts with the Word of God. Whether we wish to accept it or not, it takes time to fortify ourselves, by spiritual healing, which comes from our study of God's Word, taking in the guidance and direction from the great physicians. It requires one to submit to a continuous healing program. This program enables them to grow into a level of spiritual maturity, strengthening their immune system, so they can keep Satan at bay. How can they maintain this great spiritual renewal, rebuilding, transformation program?

The greatest medicine for spiritual sickness is the Holy Spirit. You will recall that Paul told Timothy,

2 Timothy 3:16-17 New American Standard Bible (NASB)

16 All Scripture is inspired by God and profitable for teaching, for reproof, for correction, for training in righteousness; 17 so that the man of God may be adequate, equipped for every good work.

What does this mean? The phrase "inspired by God" (Gr., *theopneustos*) literally means, "Breathed out by God." A related Greek word, *pneuma*, means "spirit." Therefore, God's Holy Spirit moved human writers, breathing upon them, in a manner of speaking, so that the end result could truthfully be called the Word of *God*, not the word of man.

2 Peter 1:21 English Standard Version (ESV)

[21] For no prophecy was ever produced by the will of man, but men spoke from God as they were carried along by the Holy Spirit.

The Greek word here translated "were carried along (ESV)," *phero*, is used in another form at Acts 27:15, 17, which describes a ship that was driven along by the wind. So the Holy Spirit, in essence, 'navigated the course' of the Bible writers. While the Spirit did not have them pick each word by dictation, it prevented the writers allowing in any information that did not convey the will and purpose of God.

Revelation 3:18 English Standard Version (ESV)

[18] I counsel you to buy from me [Jesus] gold refined by fire, so that you may be rich, and white garments so that you may clothe yourself and the shame of your nakedness may not be seen, and **salve to anoint your eyes**, so that you may see.

> **Salve to put on your eyes** recalls the miracle of Jesus in which he applied a salve of saliva mixed with dirt in healing the man born blind (John 9:1–12). On that occasion he told his

accusers, “If you were blind, you would not be guilty of sin; but now that you claim you can see, your guilt remains” (John 9:41). The Laodicean church claimed that it had spiritual insight. Would it recognize its blindness and ask for Christ’s wisdom and insight (Col. 1:9)?[16]

The Word of God is like an eye salve that is put on your eyes of understanding, assisting them to be healed, as far as their spiritual eyesight goes. This salve is far greater than any drug ever created by man. Paul tells us in the book of Hebrews, “For the word of God is living and active, sharper than any two-edged sword, piercing to the division of soul and of spirit, of joints and of marrow, and discerning the thoughts and intentions of the heart.” (Heb. 4:12, ESV) This is biblical truths, which brings about correct understanding. Jesus said that he would “ask the Father, and He will give you another Helper, that He may be with you forever.” (John 14:16)

John 14:17 New American Standard Bible (NASB)

---

[16] http://biblia.com/books/hntc87re/Page.p_61

[17] *that is* the Spirit of truth, whom the world cannot receive, because it does not see Him or know Him, *but* you know Him because He abides with you and will be in you.

God said, "Let us make man in our image, after our likeness." (Gen. 1:26) "So God created man in his own image, in the image of God he created him; male and female he created them." (Gen. 1:27) God is the designer of the human being, and is well aware of every aspect that went into that creation. Being in the image of God includes all aspects of man relative to his sphere of life. The Bible refers to the **mental powers** of intelligence by the use of the words *mind* and *conscience*. The mind is the seat of **thought** and memory: the center of consciousness that generates thoughts, feelings, ideas, and perceptions, and stores knowledge and memories.

We use the term "mind" in different ways regarding human faculty of intelligence. One such meaning is a reference to the human capacity of collecting information, to then reason on that information, so that we may draw the correct conclusions. This **thought** process is the activity of thinking, i.e., ideas, plans, conceptions, or beliefs produced by **mental activity**. For example, when studying the Bible with study tools, we might say, 'I am going to keep my *mind* on the lessons within God's Word and the study tools.' What is meant by that is, we intend to keep our mind focused, to take in the information they contain. Luke, in the book of Acts, says of the Beroeans, 'Now the Jews in Beroea were more noble as opposed to those in Thessalonica, as they received the word with all eagerness [Gr., *prothumias*, **mental readiness**], examining the Scriptures daily to see if these things were so.' (Ac 17:11) Simon J. Kistemaker in *Exposition of the Acts of the Apostles* writes,

> The reason for the openness of the Bereans lies in their receptivity to and love for God's Word. For them, the Scriptures are much more than a written scroll or book that conveys a divine message. They use the Old Testament as the touchstone of truth, so that when Paul proclaims the gospel they immediately go to God's written Word for verification. They do so, Luke adds, with great eagerness. Note well, the adjective *great* indicates that they treasure the Word of God. Luke ascribes the same diligence to the Bereans as Peter does to the Old Testament prophets, who intently and diligently searched the Word and

inquired into its meaning (1 Peter 1:10). The Bereans open the Scriptures and with ready minds learn that Jesus has fulfilled the messianic prophecies.[17]

As we said in the above, the mind is the seat of thought and **memory**. When we say something like, 'I will keep that in *mind*," we mean that we will place information into our memory for future recall. Sometimes it is good to kindle those memories to fine-tune our actions, which may have become slack. Paul wrote to Titus, saying, "Remind [Gr. *Hupomimnesko*, be you reminding] them to be submissive to rulers and authorities, to be obedient, to be ready for every good work." (Titus 3:1, ESV) We get our capacity to remember from our being created in the image of God, as Jeremiah said of him, "did not Jehovah remember them, and came it not into his mind?" (Jer. 44:21)

The human nervous system is the part of the body: the brain, the spinal cord and the vast network of nerve cells and nerve fibers picking up the perceptions of sight, hearing, smell, touch and taste, which is actually the physical tool used by our **mental powers** of intelligence to receive and convey thoughts and

---

17 http://biblia.com/books/bkrc-ac/Page.p_621

communications and control actions. It is within the human mind, where we reason on the information that we take in, to come to conclusions. Our conclusions will be correct, if we have reasoned correctly on the information that we have taken in, meaning that we will make an informed and intelligent decision. The apostle Paul told the Romans,

Romans 8:5-8 English Standard Version (ESV)

5 For those who live according to the flesh set their minds **[**Gr., *phroneo*, mental attention ("to have in mind, to think")[18]**]** on the things of the flesh, but those who live according to the Spirit set their minds on the things of the Spirit. **6** For to set the mind on the flesh is death, but to set the mind on the Spirit is life and peace. **7** For the mind that is set on the flesh is hostile to God, for it does not submit to God's law; indeed, it cannot. **8** Those who are in the flesh cannot please God.

> The mind of a human being can be set upon only one thing—either the desires of the flesh or the Spirit. The new way of life in the Spirit makes it

---

[18] Vine's Complete Expository Dictionary of Old and New Testament Words, http://biblia.com/books/tn-vines/VolumePage.V_2,_p_409

possible for the mind of the believer to be set upon **what the Spirit desires**.

Paul is not defining two categories of people here: Christians versus non-Christians, or Spirit-filled Christians versus "carnal" Christians. Rather, he is using the opposite extremes of the spectrum to illustrate two ways of living life in God's world. One way is to live it according to the desires and directives of the flesh, a way that produces hostility toward God and ultimately death. The other way is to live life according to the desires of God as revealed and empowered by his Holy Spirit, a way that leads to life and peace.

This is Paul's point. A person with his or her mind set upon the things of the flesh cannot "accept the things that come from the Spirit of God, for they are foolishness to him, and he cannot understand them, because they are spiritually discerned" (1 Cor. 2:14). All one has to do is look around societies and cultures to see the results of living life with the mind set on only that which the flesh desires. The result is not life and peace—it is death and

> destruction. But that is the easy observation to make, the one down at the far end of the spectrum. What about those who claim to be Christians who yet manifest many of the same characteristics as those who make no such claim? What are we to do with the indicators from contemporary polls that suggest the practices of "Christians" are often not much more spiritual than those who live in and of the world?[19]

If we entertain or cultivate wrong desires, mental attention, over a period, we will begin to have a mindset, which will make it easier to follow the wrong decisions. The complete pattern of conclusions, which governs our behaviors, will get so far out of sync that our mental attention will become set on "the things of the flesh." This can take place so progressive; we may not even have noticed the transition. It is like being an cool water that is warmed so slowly that we do not realize it is being brought to a boil, and we are cooking. It starts with ignoring our conscience. Each time we ignore our conscience, and listen to, watch something, drink something, do something that grates

---

[19] Holman New Testament Commentary, Romans http://biblia.com/books/hntc66ro/Ro8.9-11

against it, it grows callused, so we will eventually be unable to feel the warnings that something is wrong. If this is the case, we must reboot our system,

Romans 12:2 English Standard Version (ESV)

[2] Do not be conformed to this world, but **be transformed** by **the renewal of your mind**, that by testing you may discern what is the will of God, what is good and acceptable and perfect.

> If we do not allow ourselves to be conformed (present passive imperative of *suschematizo*), then we will not be one with (*sun*) the schemes (*schema*) of the age in which we live. While the same word for schemes is not used in the Greek text (*schema*), the same sense is implied by Paul's words in 2 Corinthians 2:11 and Ephesians 6:11 where he makes reference to Satan's schemes and strategies against believers. If Satan is the god of this world (and he is), and if the whole world lies in his power (and it does), then the believer must resist the pressure to conform morally, intellectually, and emotionally—and

ultimately behaviorally—to Satan's schemes for life. We are not to act like the "wise" of this age—those who follow their own satanically-inspired will and practices rather than God's.

And what offensive measure keeps the believer from being conformed to this present evil age? The consistent and deliberate **renewing** of the mind. To make new (Paul here uses the noun, renewal, *anakainosis*, instead of the verb *anakainoo*, to make new) is a combination of "new" (*kainos*) and "again" (*ana*). Paul uses the verb form in 2 Corinthians 4:16 where he says "we are being renewed day by day," and in Colossians 3:10where he says that the new self "is being renewed in knowledge in the image of its Creator."

Both of these uses of the verb shed light on his use of the noun here, especially the Colossians reference where he highlights a renewal of knowledge "in" (*kata*, according to) the image of God. In other words, believers are coming out of Satan's domain where lies and depravity are the language and currency and depraved minds (Rom. 1:28) are the norm. Therefore, our minds must be renewed in knowledge according to the image of God, not the age in which Satan rules.

The ongoing, repetitive nature of the renewal is drawn from the present passive imperative of *metamorphoo*, to change form. It is from this Greek word that our "metamorphosis" derives—"a transformation; a marked change in appearance, character, condition, or function" (*American Heritage Dictionary*). The English definition describes perfectly the "metamorphosis" which took place before the disciples' eyes as Jesus was transfigured (*metamorphoo*) before them: "His face shone like the sun, and his clothes became as white as the light" (Matt. 17:2), "whiter than anyone in the world could bleach them" (Mark 9:3).[20]

Colossians 3:9-10 English Standard Version (ESV)

9 Do not lie to one another, seeing that you have put off the old self with its

---

[20] Holman New Testament Commentary http://biblia.com/books/hntc66ro/Page.p_366

practices [10] and have **put on the new self**, which is being renewed in knowledge after the image of its creator.

Perverted passions, hot tempers, and sharp tongues are to be removed as part of the life-transformation process. These things, along with **[lying] to each other**, are not appropriate behavior for our new life in Christ. The remnants of the former lifestyle are to be discarded **since [we] have taken off [our] old self with its practices**. What is the **old self** (literally "old man") and the **new self** (literally "the new")? The "old man" refers to more than an individual condition ("sinful nature") and also has a corporate aspect. The corporate aspect of "the new" (man) is unmistakably seen in verse 11. What has been **put off** and what has been **put on?** Our former associations, the old humanity has been **put off**, and we now have a new association, the new community. As members of the new community, we are to conduct ourselves in ways which will enhance harmony in the community. Notice how the sins mentioned in the previous verses disrupt community and damage human relationships.

As individuals, and as believing communities, our objective is to be a part of the transformation process of **being renewed in knowledge in the image of its Creator** (Christ). Within the new community all barriers are abolished. Distinctions which normally divide people—racial (**Greek or Jew**); religious (**circumcised or uncircumcised**); cultural (**barbarian** or **Scythian**); social (**slave or free**)—no longer have significance. The reason human categories no longer matter is that **Christ is all**, which means Christ is central and supreme. Our relationship with him is really all that matters. Unity within the community is based on the fact that Christ **is in all**. He indwells **all** believers and permeates all our relationships. This does not mean that people cease to be Jew or Greek, slave or free, etc. It does mean that within the new community those distinctions don't matter. The false teachers at Colosse were fond of dividing people into categories—elite

> versus ordinary, spiritual versus not so spiritual. The truth is, all believers are equal; all believers are to discard any and all behaviors and attitudes which are inappropriate for our new life.[21]

As you know, we can have different attitudes of mind, like being high-minded, meaning having or showing high moral principles. Then, we could be humble-minded, meaning one who is modest and unassuming in attitude and behavior. The latter was the mindset of Christ, which Paul spoke about to the Philippians. Paul exhorted, "Have this mind among yourselves, which is yours in Christ Jesus." (Phil 2:5) Peter also says, "Since therefore Christ suffered in the flesh, arm yourselves with the same way of thinking." (1 Pet 4:1) The word *spirit* can refer to one's will or sense of self, or somebody's personality or temperament. This is largely influenced by the mind.

Proverbs 25:28 American Standard Version (ASV)

28 He whose spirit [personality or temperament] is without restraint is like a city that is broken down and without walls.

---

[21] Holman New Testament Commentary: http://biblia.com/books/hntc69ga/Col3.12-14

However, we are blessed from another loving gift, another mental power from our heavenly Father at creation of Adam and Eve. Getting back to Genesis 1:27 that says, "God created man in his own image, in the image of God he created him; male and female he created them," which means that man is born with a moral nature, which creates within him a conscience that reflects God's moral values. (Rom 2:14-15) It acts as a moral law within. Even in imperfection, we are born with a measure of that conscience, which can be developed toward good or bad. A Christian conscience is developed by the Word of God.

Titus 1:15 English Standard Version (ESV)

15 To the pure [persons with a conscience guided by the Bible], all things are pure, but to the defiled and unbelieving, nothing is pure; but both their minds [mental power] and their consciences are defiled.

We have to appreciate and realize that even after we take on the new person that Paul spoke of, as well as the mind of Christ, we will still be affected by our inborn leanings of a sinful nature. Really, there is a battle because waging between the two.

Romans 7:21-25 Lexham English Bible (LEB)

[21] Consequently, I find the principle with me, the one who wants to do good, that evil is present with me.[22] [22] For I joyfully agree with the law of God in my inner person, [23] but I observe another law in my members, at war with the law of my mind and making me captive to the law of sin that exists in my members. [24] Wretched man *that* I *am*! Who will rescue me from this body of death? [25] Thanks *be*[23] to God through Jesus Christ our Lord! So then, I myself with my mind am enslaved to the law of God, but with my flesh *I am enslaved* to the law of sin.

The good news is that if a person is walking with Christ and according to Scripture, he will no longer be a slave to sin. The sinful leaning will be there, but as long as it is nit fed, it will not dominate his life. He will no longer have a life that deeds the beast, such as inappropriate music, television, internet viewing, associations, thinking, and so on. This will give him a clean conscience before God, knowing that he now has a righteous standing, and all his past has been forgiven, cast behind the back of God. There may come times in his life when his sinful nature will attempt to reassert itself, and he will

---

[22] Or "in me"

[23] Some manuscripts have "But thanks be"

have to take steps of dismissing any wrongful thinking, replacing it with rational Scriptural thinking, as well as intensive prayer, even speaking with a spiritually mature one within the congregation.

CHAPTER 16 Now is the Day of Salvation

CHAPTER 16

We are still living in "the day of salvation," which is a good thing, meaning, an opportunity at eternal live for us, and our loved ones. Paul wrote to the Corinthians,

2 Corinthians 6:1-2 Holman Christian Standard Bible (HCSB)

6 Working together with Him, we also appeal to you, "Don't receive God's grace in vain." 2 For He says:

I heard you in an acceptable time, and I helped you in the day of salvation.

Look, now is the acceptable time; now is the day of salvation.

Below is a quote from David E. Garland, out of the *New American Commentary* (Vol. 29, p. 304)

> "As God's fellow workers" is a bold statement that translates one word in Greek "working together" *(synergountes)*. The verb has no object, but most translations assume that it refers to working together with God. Paul could be referring to his

human coworkers; but since this phrase follows 5:20, where he asserts that God gave him a ministry of reconciliation and that God makes his appeal through him, he surely has in mind working with God.[24] This statement reminds them of his divine commission and authority while also asserting that what he does is God's work, not his. Working together with God means that he sets out to accomplish God's objectives, not his own. In the context that objective concerns reconciliation. God sent Christ as his agent to make reconciliation possible. God uses ambassadors like Paul to continue that agenda—to call people to be reconciled to God, to make known that God does not count their sins against them and that God loves them and yearns for them to repent.

Yet Paul directs his call for reconciliation specifically to the Corinthians (5:20), and he implores

---

[24] Paul identifies Timothy as God's coworker in 1 Thess 3:2. Paul also refers to Apollos and himself as God's coworkers (NIV, "God's fellow workers") in 1 Cor 3:9, although Furnish understands the term to mean "coworkers for God" (*II Corinthians*, 341).

them not to receive God's grace in vain *(eis kenon)*.[25] The grace refers to God's reconciling work in Christ. Paul apparently took this warning to heart himself. He wrote to the Corinthians about his call to be an apostle: "But by the grace of God I am what I am, and his grace to me was not without effect *[kenē]*. No, I worked harder than all of them—yet not I, but the grace of God that was with me" (1 Cor 15:10). He assumes that they have received God's grace, but what would make it all for nothing? Lapide cites Anselm: "He receives grace into a vacuum … who does not work with it, who does not give it his heart, and who, through sloth, makes that grace ineffectual, by not doing all that he can to express it in good works."[26] This interpretation makes this statement an applicable warning to all Christians, but Paul has something more specific in view for the Corinthians than allowing God's grace to produce fruit in their Christian life.

---

25 This is the only finite verb in this section (vv. 1–10, aside from the parenthesis in v. 2).

26 Lapide, *The Great Commentary of Cornelius à Lapide*, 84.

The admonition that follows in 6:14–7:1 suggests that their continuing association with idols would cause their faith to founder on the rocks.[27]

Paul explains the gravity of the situation with a verbatim quotation from Isa 49:8 (quoting the LXX, not the Hebrew text). The acceptable time ("the time of my favor") is when God mercifully answered prayer and acted for Israel's salvation. Paul then provides a commentary on what this passage means now. It refers to something even greater than the return from exile in Babylon. The "now" refers to the eschatological change of the ages inaugurated by Christ's death (see Rom 3:21,26; 5:9, 11; 6:22; 7:6; 8:1). The day of salvation applies to the deliverance from sin's captivity through Jesus'cross and resurrection. The acceptable time ("the time of God's favor," NIV) refers to God's timetable that completely ignores what is acceptable or timely to humans. The implication would be clear to those in

---

[27] See further J. Gundry-Volf, Paul and Perseverance: Staying in and Falling Away, WUNT 2/37 (Tübingen: Mohr [Siebeck]) 277–80.

Paul's age who were familiar with the ancient cliché "to seize the day." To become acceptable to God, one must accept God's offer of reconciliation. Yet hearing the promise is no guarantee that the promise will be received. They must obey as long as it is still called "Today" (Heb 3:13).[28]

"The day of salvation" is **now** about 1,980 years from the death and resurrection of Jesus Christ. When this day will end is not something the Bible discloses. It could be tomorrow, next year, five years, or fifty years, maybe even one hundred and fifty years. Nevertheless, while the window of opportunity is open, let us continue our own walk with God, being declared righteous until the end. (Matt 24:13) We can also use thus brief period of time in which we have the opportunity, as coworkers of God, to help save other persons.

We are living in this **"acceptable time,"** not for our own salvation, but for others, who are receptive to the Word of God. This means that we are willing to make sacrifices of ourselves in this acceptable time, knowing that it is so very minuscule, when compared to an eternity that is to come. Someone loved God

---

[28] http://biblia.com/books/nac29/Page.p_305

and neighbor enough to buy out the time to bring us the Gospel, now we must pay it forward to as many as we can, before this window of opportunity closes.

The Time that Remains

When we think of the time that remains in this "day of salvation," it is a very brief period. That is, when we compare it to the two millenniums that have passed since its beginning. We should feel the rush of excitement, knowing that it could be any day, any week, and year of our life, in which Christ returns. This makes our lives ever so important in the grand scheme of things. Therefore, it is highly important that we follow the counsel given by the Son,

Matthew 7:21-23 English Standard Version (ESV)

[21] "Not everyone who says to me, 'Lord, Lord,' will enter the kingdom of heaven, but the one who does the will of my Father who is in heaven.[22] On that day many will say to me, 'Lord, Lord, did we not prophesy in your name, and cast out demons in your name, and do many mighty works in your name?'[23] And then will I declare to them, 'I never knew you; depart from me, you workers of lawlessness.'

Yes, we want to do the will of the Father, which also includes being obedient to the Son.

Matthew 24:14 English Standard Version (ESV)

[14] And this gospel of the kingdom will be proclaimed throughout the whole world as a testimony to all nations, and then the end will come.

Matthew 28:19-20 English Standard Version (ESV)

[19] Go therefore and make disciples of all nations … teaching them to observe all that I have commanded you. And behold, I am with you always, to the end of the age."

Acts 1:8 English Standard Version (ESV)

[8] But you will receive power when the Holy Spirit has come upon you, and you will be my witnesses in Jerusalem and in all Judea and Samaria, and to the end of the earth."

May we buy out the time in this present age, so we can carry out the one Great command that Jesus gave us, namely, bringing others into the fold of Christianity, before the closing of the "acceptable time"?

Bibliography

Akin, Daniel L. *The New American Commentary: 1, 2, 3 John*. Nashville, TN: Broadman & Holman , 2001.

Anders, Max. *Holman New Testament Commentary: vol. 8, Galatians, Ephesians, Philippians, Colossians*. Nashville, TN: Broadman & Holman Publishers, 1999.

—. *Holman Old Testament Commentary - Proverbs* . Nashville: B&H Publishing, 2005.

Anders, Max, and Trent Butler. *Holman Old Testament Commentary: Isaiah*. Nashiville, TN: B&H Publishing, 2002.

Andrews, Edward D. *THE EVANGELISM HANDBOOK: How All Christians Can Effectively Share God's Word in Their Community*. Cambridge: Christian Publishing House, 2013.

Arnold, Clinton E. *Zondervan Illustrated Bible Backgrounds Commentary Volume 2: John, Acts.* . Grand Rapids, MI: Zondervan, 2002.

—. *Zondervan Illustrated Bible Backgrounds Commentary Volume 3: Romans to*

Philemon. Grand Rapids: Zondervan, 2002.

—. *Zondervan Illustrated Bible Backgrounds Commentary Volume 4: Hebrews to Revelation*. Grand Rapids, MI: Zondervan, 2002.

—. *Zondervan Illustrated Bible Backgrounds Commentary: Matthew, Mark, Luke, vol. 1*. Grand Rapids, MI: Zondervan, 2002.

Blomberg, Craig. *The New American Commentary: Matthew* . Nashville, TN : Broadman & Holman Publishers, 2001.

Boa, Kenneth, and Kruidenier. *Holman New Testament Commentary: Romans*. Nashville: Broadman & Holman, 2000.

Borchert, Gerald L. *The New American Commentary: John 1-11* . Nashville, TN: Broadman & Holman Publishers, 2001.

Brand, Chad, Charles Draper, and England Archie. *Holman Illustrated Bible Dictionary: Revised, Updated and Expanded*. Nashville, TN: Holman, 2003.

Buter, Trent C. *Holman New Testament Commentary: Luke*. Nashville, TN: Broadman & Holman Publishers, 2000.

Easley, Kendell H. *Holman New Testament Commentary, vol. 12, Revelation.* (Nashville, TN: Broadman & Holman Publishers, 1998.

Elwell, Walter A, and Philip Wesley Comfort. *Tyndale Bible Dictionary.* Wheaton, Ill: Tyndale House Publishers, 2001.

Freedman, David Noel, Allen C. Myers, and Astrid B. Beck. *Eerdmans Dictionary of the Bible* . Grand Rapids, Mich.: W.B. Eerdmans , 2000.

Gangel, Kenneth O. *Holman New Testament Commentary, vol. 4, John* . Nashville, TN: Broadman & Holman Publishers, 2000.

Geisler, Norman, and David Geisler. *CONVERSATION EVANGELISM: How to Listen and Speak So You Can Be Heard.* Eugene: Harvest House Publishers, 2009.

Larson, Knute. *Holman New Testament Commentary, vol. 9, I & II Thessalonians, I & II Timothy, Titus, Philemon.* Nashville, TN: Broadman & Holman Publishers, 2000.

Lea, Thomas D, and Hayne P Griffin. *The New American Commentary: 1, 2 Timothy,*

Titus . Nashville: Broadman & Holman, 2001.

Lea, Thomas D. *Holman New Testament Commentary: Vol. 10, Hebrews, James.* Nashville, TN: Broadman & Holman Publishers, 1999.

Martin, Glen S. *Holman Old Testament Commentary: Numbers.* Nashville: Broadman & Holman Publishers, 2002.

Mayers, Mark K. *Christianity Confronts Culture: A Strategy for Crosscultural Evangelism.* Grand Rapids : Zondervan, 1987.

McCue, Rolland. *Promises Unfulfilled: The Failed Strategy of Modern Evangelism.* Greenville, SC: Ambassador Group, 2004.

McRaney, William. *The Art of Personal Evangelism.* Nashville: Broadman & Holman, 2003.

Melick, Richard R. *The New American Commentary: Philippians, Colissians, Philemon, electronic ed., Logos Library System* . Nashville: Broadman & Holman Publishers, 2001.

Mounce, Robert H. *The New American Commentary: Vol. 27 Romans.* Nashville,

TN: Broadman & Holman Publishers, 2001.

Mounce, William D. *Mounce's Complete Expository Dictionary of Old & New Testament Words.* Grand Rapids, MI: Zondervan, 2006.

Pratt Jr, Richard L. *Holman New Testament Commentary: I & II Corinthians, vol. 7.* Nashville: Broadman & Holman Publishers, 2000.

Reid, Alvin. *Introduction to Evangelism.* Nashville: Boardman & Holmes , 1998.

Stein, Robert H. *The New American Commentary: Luke.* Nashville, TN: Broadman & Holman , 2001, c1992.

Vine, W E. *Vine's Expository Dictionary of Old and New Testament Words.* Nashville: Thomas Nelson, 1996.

Walls, David, and Max Anders. *Holman New Testament Commentary: I & II Peter, I, II & III John, Jude.* Nashville: Broadman & Holman Publishers, 1996.

Weber, Stuart K. *Holman New Testament Commentary, vol. 1, Matthew.* Nashville, TN: Broadman & Holman Publishers, 2000.

Wood, D R W. *New Bible Dictionary (Third Edition)*. Downers Grove: InterVarsity Press, 1996.

Previous Volumes of The Christian Evangelist

www.ingramcontent.com/pod-product-compliance
Lightning Source LLC
Chambersburg PA
CBHW032000040426
42448CB00006B/435

* 9 7 8 0 6 9 2 2 4 1 3 9 4 *